Multilingualism in the Early `

Multilingualism in the Early Years is a highly accessible text that examines the political, theoretical, ideological and practical issues involved in the education of children speaking two or more languages. Drawing on current research and thinking about the advantages and disadvantages of being multilingual, Smidt uses powerful case studies to reveal how language or languages are acquired. She explores language in terms of who shares it, its relationship to class, culture, power, identity and thinking, and its fascinating role as it moves from the personal to the public and political. More specifically the book studies:

- what it means to be bilingual through an analysis of the language histories submitted by a range of people;
- how language/s define people;
- a brief history of minority education in the UK;
- how practitioners and teachers can best support all young children as learners whilst they continue to use their first languages and remain part of and partners in their communities and cultures;
- being bilingual: an advantage or a disadvantage?
- the impact of multilingualism on children's educational and life chances.

Multilingualism in the Early Years is a really useful text for practitioners working with multilingual children, as well as any student undertaking courses in early childhood education.

Sandra Smidt is a writer and consultant in early years education.

Multilingualism in the Early Years

Extending the limits of our world

Sandra Smidt

Routledge
Taylor & Francis Group

LONDON AND NEW YORK

First published 2016
by Routledge
2 Park Square, Milton Park, Abingdon, Oxon OX14 4RN

and by Routledge
711 Third Avenue, New York, NY 10017

Routledge is an imprint of the Taylor & Francis Group, an informa business

British Library Cataloguing in Publication Data
A catalogue record for this book is available from the British Library

Library of Congress Cataloging in Publication Data
A catalog record for this book has been requested

ISBN: 978-1-138-94244-8 (hbk)
ISBN: 978-1-138-94245-5 (pbk)
ISBN: 978-1-315-67315-8 (ebk)

Typeset in Bembo
by Keystroke, Station Road, Codsall, Wolverhampton
Printed in Great Britain by Ashford Colour Press Ltd

MIX
Paper from
responsible sources
FSC   FSC® C011748
www.fsc.org

This book is dedicated to Adrine, Alfredo, Anne, Carmen, Carol, Cleo, Dario, Fatih, Hong-Bich, Janos, Jill, Marion, Marisa, Mellie, Mike, Raymonde, Rosa, Snoeks, Toula and Beate, whose story appears below:

Beate Planskoy has an extraordinary family history – sadly not because it was rare, but extraordinary for her ability to deal with all that happened to her and her family and to build on it. You will guess within the first three sentences that she was one of those fleeing fascism in the last century. She and her siblings arrived in London from Berlin on a Kinder Transport in April 1939.

My family lived in Germany for many generations. They and their parents and grandparents spoke German at home. When we came to England in April 1939, my brother, sister and I went to school and picked up English as fast as possible. My parents who, by a miracle, managed to join us in London on 31 August – two days before the war started – had reasonably good English based on their secondary education. We then spoke English in public and German at home. (This was during World War II.) Gradually my generation spoke English more and more often and eventually always to each other. To my parents we continued to write in and speak German a lot of the time.

My nephews and nieces, all born in England, speak only English and so does the next generation.

My husband's linguistic history may be of interest. He spoke five European languages, all learned as a child, completely fluently. Russian: was his native language. He was born and grew up in Russia; Polish: he spent many school holidays staying with Polish relatives in Poland; German: nanny who knew little Russian and only spoke to him in German; French: good school tuition plus a French tutor at home; English: a Scottish grandmother who never mastered the Russian language. She always spoke English with him.

After he emigrated from Russia, he studied and worked for some years in Germany, France and the United States before settling in England. Whichever language he spoke, he retained his unmistakable Russian accent.

Contents

Preface

This book has its roots in an earlier book – *Supporting Multilingual Learners in the Early Years* (Smidt, 2008) – which arose out of my awareness that many of those working in multilingual early years settings and classrooms knew little about how to communicate with and/or teach those having languages other than or additional to English. The book, written in 2008, was a slim one, aimed particularly at the growing body of those training to be teaching assistants, early years practitioners, teachers, childcare workers and others. The tone of writing was designed to be non-academic and the intention to make some difficult concepts accessible to all. That book is clearly now very out of date and the world a different place. This book does not seek to replace the earlier one, but rather to add to it.

As I started to think about the book I remembered some of the many bilingual or multilingual people I have met and who have talked to me about the languages they speak and I decided to send a short email to them, asking four very simple questions:

- What languages did your grandparents speak?
- What languages did your parents speak?
- What languages do you speak?
- What languages do your children (if you have any) speak?

One of those to whom I sent these questions was Marisa, the partner of my brother. I have never met her but my brother has talked about her and her languages and cultures and so I sent her the email. She not only replied but passed it on to many of her multilingual friends. The language histories that emerged are at the very heart of this book. They provide the opening section and then occur as examples or illustrations or reminders, and because they have been written by many people there are many voices in this book.

This book is made up of four sections that take the reader from the very personal tone of the first section to the more formal tone of the final section.

Section I: The bilingual child in the home and family

This section looks at the bilingual child in the home and family. It consists of four chapters, as follows:

- *Chapter 1: My language/languages: Language histories* – made of a series of the personal language histories described above followed by a summary of what you might have learned from your reading of these.
- *Chapter 2: Being bilingual* – which draws on what being bilingual means to those who are and to those who are not.
- *Chapter 3: How language can define you* – which looks at what bilingual people say about how they are defined by their languages and cultures. This is followed up later in the book.
- *Chapter 4: How we acquire our first and subsequent languages.*

Section II: From the home and local community to the classroom or setting

This section moves the focus from the home and local community to the classroom or setting. It is made up of three chapters, which are:

- *Chapter 5: Language/languages in the school curriculum*
- *Chapter 6: Why young children should use their first language throughout their early years*
- *Chapter 7: A brief history of minority education in the UK.*

Section III: Supporting children in classes and settings to learn and remain attached to their languages and cultures

Here we begin to consider many of the issues about how practitioners and teachers can best support all children in classes and settings to learn and remain attached to their languages and cultures. It is made up of three chapters, as follows:

- *Chapter 8: Making sense of a new world*
- *Chapter 9: Understanding multimodality and translanguaging in early education*
- *Chapter 10: The threat of a good example: Celebrating and supporting young bilingual learners* – at the end of this chapter there is a section called 'The implications for practitioners' since it is here that 'advice' is offered.

Section IV: Moving from the personal to the public

In this last section we are looking at things remote from the everyday lives of young children and their families but things that affect their education and life chances. So we go from the personal to the public. There are five chapters in this section, which are:

- *Chapter 11: Which children? Whose rights?*
- *Chapter 12: Performing culture*
- *Chapter 13: Language and identity*
- *Chapter 14: Preserving language and culture*
- *Chapter 15: Pedagogy, politics and poverty.*

At the end of the book you will find the following:

- a bibliography of the sources and resources cited in it;
- an index of the terms and names in the book.

Section I

The bilingual child in the home and family

'I'm missing the practice and the lightness and spirit of the language'
Cleo Ganz

Does it surprise you that, in many countries around the world, multilingualism is the norm? There are more than 20 states or countries that have more than one *official language*. India, for example, has 19 official languages. In my birth country of South Africa there are 11 official languages. And apart from official languages there are the other languages of the people. The term *heritage language* has been coined to describe any language a child learns/uses within the home that is not the official or *majority language* of the country. This may be synonymous with *mother tongue* or the first language the child learns. In some of the literature this first language is written as L1. And where reference is made to a second language acquired this is L2. For generations, people all over the world, confronted by poverty, war, lack of resources, paucity of jobs, poor living conditions and discrimination, have been and continue to be forced into emigrating in their search for a decent sustainable life. Those of us privileged to be in the developed world encounter more and more people coming to live here in our developed countries. In our schools and settings we will continue to welcome children speaking languages other than our official language of English. Since this is, and will continue to be, the reality, the question is raised as to whether we should focus entirely on ensuring these children learn to speak, read and write English (which they will surely do as they learn and play and live in a society where English dominates), or should we ensure that they are encouraged to learn English whilst maintaining the language or languages they already know and that are a link to their past and their culture? That is the pressing question we ask.

We start with the personal and the local as we set out to consider the implications of speaking, reading, writing, learning, teaching, loving, living and communicating in more than one language. So this section will focus primarily on individual learners as the starting point for examining the limits of our worlds.

Chapter 1

My language/languages

Language histories

As I have already written earlier in this book, my starting point was inviting people whom I know speak more than one language to tell more about their linguistic heritage. I was surprised and highly delighted by how seriously these questions were taken and how much interest they stirred in the people responding. Many sent my email on to others. All responses are to be found in this book – some in their entirety and some in the form of shorter extracts. Some have been slightly reworded to make sure they are clear. All raise issues that will be discussed in the book. Others illustrate points being made or offer touching or illuminating insights into the lives of others. As you read through them you might like to keep these questions in mind.

- Did all of these people move country?
- Did they leave for similar reasons?
- Did they hear more than one language as part of everyday life from birth?
- Did they lose their first language by choice?
- Did you feel that they rejoice in their linguistically rich lives?
- Did any of them suggest that they had lost something in terms of culture, history, opportunities, abilities?
- Is there any indication of the effect of formal education on their use of languages or of their language on their education?
- And what happened to the original first language by the time you get to the children or grandchildren?

We will return to these at the end of the chapter.

The first case history comes from Janos, the husband of my friend Hazel Abel. I have known Hazel for many years and she shares with me a passion for chamber music (which is, for both of us, another language) and an interest in early childhood education. Janos was born in Hungary and then, like so many people, had to leave his home country – in his case, as a refugee.

His parents were peasants and he had to leave school at the age of 14. Here is what he wrote:

> They only spoke Hungarian. One of my grandfathers must have known Spanish because he went to South America. He made money there and when he returned to Hungary he bought land to farm in the North East of Hungary.
>
> My parents spoke Hungarian and didn't learn any other language.
>
> I grew up speaking Hungarian in Budapest. When I was evacuated to my grandparents in the country I was self-conscious about my city accent.
>
> When I became a refugee I went to a coal miners' hostel in Scotland where we were given English lessons every day. These were paid for by the coal board because we were going to become coal miners.
>
> I came to England after a year, where I worked for British Rail; I continued to learn English from reading and studying. My plan was to learn ten words a day!
>
> I lived with a few Hungarians during this time but I wanted to speak only English. I was very pleased when my friends agreed to speak only English. Then I left England for Paris. I could not speak a word of French but I wanted to live in France so that I could learn French. I spent 2 years in Paris studying on my own and tried to speak whenever I could. It was hard because so many of the young people had learnt English and wanted to practise on me. During the second year I went to the Alliance Française for French language lessons. I liked the assimil direct method (which is similar to programmes like Linguaphone) so I got records out of the library. I had the ambition to learn German and Italian as well but I didn't manage to get there. I met Hazel!
>
> Ever since getting married I have spoken only English except with my parents when they visited and when visiting Hungary on holiday. My children speak English. I took two of my daughters to Hungary when they were 6 and 8 years old. The elder daughter learnt quite a lot of Hungarian from her grandparents and has always enjoyed learning languages at school, evening classes and when she went to live abroad. The younger daughter was totally overwhelmed by the experience and remembers only one sentence of Hungarian 'hol van a mask zokni?' 'Where is the other sock?', or to be more precise, 'where is the other half of my pair of socks?'! She learnt French at school and lived in Paris for a while but she found it hard to learn a language. Now it is difficult for me to speak Hungarian. I was 19 when I left and my language then was probably not advanced enough for discussions in subjects that I enjoy talking about now – for example economics, philosophy.

The second language history comes from Raymonde Sneddon, a dear colleague, friend and often a role model for me. We retired on the same day from the same university and celebrated by talking about our lives, which we discovered had touched without us realising this. She, too, has lived and learned in many places. Here is what she says:

> I am a French English bilingual.
>
> My French grandparents lived in Aix-en-Provence in France and spoke exclusively French, and my Scottish grandparents lived on the Isle of Bute and spoke only English.
>
> My mother was brought up in Scotland speaking only English. She went on to study German in night classes. After she met my father during the war, she learned to speak French.
>
> My father was brought up in France speaking only French, but learned English when he joined the Royal Navy during the war.
>
> Both my parents became fully bilingual and biliterate over the years.
>
> I was born on the Isle of Bute. I learned both English and French as a child: English first, then French when the family moved to France when I was 2 years old. My mother always spoke English to me; my father both languages, and everyone else in my environment spoke French. My mother reports that for almost a year at the age of 4 I insisted on answering her in French, but I got over that and never lost the use of English. I was educated all over the place, mainly in France and Francophone countries, with short spells in Scotland (aged 5) and New Zealand (aged 15). When I was 11, in a lycée in France, I was ridiculed by the English teacher for my Scottish accent when I spoke English. For the rest of my school career I hid the fact that I was bilingual, making just enough mistakes to remain undetected. I learned Latin and German at school. Wishing to redress my French language dominance I went on to study English literature and language at Edinburgh University.
>
> I spoke some French at home with my first child, but as his autism developed he lost the use of speech altogether. Concerned to avoid confusion (and not knowing what I know now) I stopped using French to him. This impacted on his younger brother who heard little French in the home. While both children learned to understand some French during family visits to their cousins in Aix, my youngest never became fluent. This he now regrets and has asked me to ensure that his children become bilingual. As a regularly baby-sitting grandmother, I have spoken entirely French to his two daughters since they were born. The eldest, at 22 months, has a substantial understanding of French words and spontaneously uses some in the right context (to me). She appears to be well aware that her mémé says things differently.

I met Hong-Bich Vernon on a painting course (yet another language) in France a year ago. She adds another dimension when she explains the intricacies of her family's language history.

My grandparents spoke Vietnamese in Vietnam and when we moved to the US it was Vietnamese at home and English outside of the home. In Vietnam my father was educated in a school where both French and Vietnamese were the medium of instruction. When I was a little girl he sang French songs to us and we listened to French language radio. My mother spoke only Vietnamese, and learned only a little English, largely because she had to take care of ten children plus a husband. In school in Vietnam I was introduced to both French and English, but I concentrated on English as a foreign language. My courses with the exception of English were all taught in Vietnamese. As a result of the war, American television was available in Vietnam and some of the programmes were American with Vietnamese voiceovers. We also heard both American and French music on the radio. We owned a bookstore with Vietnamese books, but we also sold English language books.

My father also speaks French. My father worked on and retired from the Vietnamese rail road company and in his youth the company was run by the French, and so he spoke French at work as well as Vietnamese. He is 94 years old today and he still reads books in French.

Our family left Vietnam on 27 April 1975 as refugees and we entered the United States at a time when none of the current system of language learning support and special programmes existed. We were all thrust into school and work in a situation of sink or swim, and so we all learned to swim in English as best we could.

As my husband is American and does not speak Vietnamese, we speak English at home. I speak Vietnamese to all my siblings, English to my nieces and nephews who were all born and raised in the US. They speak English to one another. Besides Vietnamese and English, I have also learned French, Thai and Malay, although none of them as fluently as I speak English.

Our two sons were born in Switzerland, and we had the ambition for them to be bilingual in Vietnamese and English. I spoke Vietnamese to them when they were very young. They understood but never spoke back in Vietnamese, possibly because at that time we were not part of a Vietnamese community and they never had the chance or need to use the language. I read to them in English as there weren't any Vietnamese books around at that time, and finally we just concentrated on English. I feel a little bit bad for not consistently speaking Vietnamese to them, but it was getting too complicated. They are, however, bilingual (English and French) at school, but now we mainly speak English at home.

Marion Iacopucci is a dear friend who lives half the time in England and half the time in Italy. She, like me, was born in South Africa but she left the country with her family when she was a small child and all her schooling took place in the UK. Here is her language history unedited because she has such a personal and particular way of writing. It may not be strictly grammatical, breaking rules in many places, but the meaning shines out.

My paternal grandparents: He, German born, spoke German and English (lived in Texas before it was in the US). She, born in Danzig, was Prussia, now Polish Gdanzk, German mother tongue, English and French (Polish ??? don't think so). moved to New York after Bergen Belsen. Have a lovely poem my granddad wrote my grandma in English in Bergen Belsen.

Maternal grandparents: He, East Europe somewhere??? ended up in South Africa, languages, English, German and ?? She, born in a German speaking part of what is now Lithuania, German mother tongue, English from early childhood in South Africa.

Parents: Gerhard, born Germany, South Africa in 1933, German and English, tried for a little Spanish while living in Lanzarote, and hardly any Italian, perhaps too deaf by then. Hilda, born South Africa, English, I suppose some Afrikaans, boh! understood German well (perhaps they spoke it at home in early childhood?) and spoke it when necessary, never spoke much Italian, but understood quite a bit.

Me: English is where my head and imagination and place in the world reside. I was taught Afrikaans for 5 years, and don't remember a word, French (5 years) and Latin (2 years) at school. Was totally at home in Italian while Vincenzo (my husband) was alive, but now it takes me a week or so to lose my English accent and remember how to speak it. But losing words and fluency in both languages.

Dario, my son: Bilingual English and Italian. But still has an Italian intonation. He did Latin for 5 years. Has a tin ear, and has never got on with Mandarin (despite living and working Hong Kong for years) – all those tonal meanings and sheer laziness.

Cleo, my daughter: Trilingual. Italian, English, German, though she would say she no longer speaks any language properly. Did Spanish for 3 years, and Latin and Greek for a while. Her English is my English, which she feels keenly is out of date, she does make some grammatical mistakes in German. Her accents are indistinguishable from native.

Both kids are not very good at English spelling.

Grandchildren: German mother tongue, all have really excellent results in English at school. Lisa understands everything, but I have never heard her say a word in English, did Latin and, I think, is doing Spanish now. She speaks reasonable Italian, as does Gioia who is very fluent in English, having spent a term at the Steiner school in Hereford, also learns and hates Russian at school. Ben understands English quite well and gives it a good go in speaking. Ditto Italian. Don't know his school languages apart from English. Sofia, 18 months. Hears mainly Italian. Understands it very well, but doesn't speak yet. Also responds to some English. One of the reasons for going to Hong Kong Katy (her mother) told me today is so that she will grow up bilingual with English. Also may learn Mandarin.

Knowing Marion and all her family so well I find this a moving account of what happens to people when they move for one reason or another. Imagine having a poem written in English by your grandfather for your grandmother when they were suffering the intolerable conditions of Bergen Belsen.

I met Carol O'Brien, like Hazel, through a shared passion for chamber music and learned that she is something of a linguist. Here is her fascinating account, in which she is the first to talk about the glamour of becoming someone else through using another language as well as about accent.

My paternal grandparents were Australian and lived in Australia until they were in their early twenties, then in England. They spoke English, but with an Australian accent.

My maternal grandparents lived in São Paulo and both spoke very little Portuguese, and my grandmother at least (I never knew my grandfather) with an execrable accent. Otherwise English – and she came 'home' when her husband died in Brazil, with her three children.

My father spoke English. My mother spoke Portuguese with the Brazilian servants as a small child; English for the rest of the time. She read languages at Oxford, and spoke both French and Spanish beautifully.

I speak English. Was sent as a 9-year-old to spend a summer in France and came back speaking fluent French; and subsequently learned Spanish. (I was one of three girls doing German at A level, but the other two were German with whom I couldn't keep up, so decided I wanted to do Spanish instead! To my surprise they let me, though I was the only girl in the school doing Spanish, and had to go in to Oxford for lessons. I subsequently spent a summer in a Spanish family and later worked as a hotel room-service telephonist in Spain.)

I always felt, when speaking a foreign language, that it was glamorous and romantic and exhilarating – like being someone else – and loved it. One thing that amazes me is to discover I still know the words for something, learned almost 60 years ago, and probably never used since (e.g. walking down the street recently I saw a bird-cage and remembered it was in Spanish a jaúl). Where on earth do these words live in my brain???

My step-brother married a German (from West Berlin), and she always spoke German to their two children, though they always replied in English. Her English is perfect (and her Finnish very good too), and when I asked her if she ever missed German she thought for a bit and then said 'Only a few particular words – like the German for goose fat.'

Several of the other authors of the language histories wrote about how speaking a particular language can allow the speaker to adopt a different persona. Marion added this to her language history, which you have already read:

> When I first went to stay in Italy in 1965 my name quickly became Mary (Meri), which was easier and less unusual for people to say and remember. But Meri wasn't quite Marion. I do think there were changes in my behaviour and the way I presented myself: Meri was adapting to an entirely new and different cultural setting. Rural backwater, no other foreigner. And although much of my London strange behaviour and clothing and lack of language was mostly nicely forgiven because as a foreigner I didn't know any better, I did make a conscious effort to conform and fit in as much as I felt I could without becoming an outright world class actress. For many years I bit my tongue (honest injun!) and most people didn't have the faintest idea of who I was – really the appendage (concubine, according to my sisters-in-law) of Vincenzo who everybody knew. Vincenzo was an inventive and imaginative blasphemer; it had no particular meaning for me, so I never did and it took me a long while to learn to swear, which was much more my medium, but I was careful where I used it.

> Later the local scene changed, and Bagni started to emerge into the modern world, of which I could then return to being an exemplar, with a less socially dual personality. Vincenzo was a great help and support through all of this, both because he always lived and let live, and also because he was so utterly untypical of his native environment himself. We jointly loudly rang all the wrong bells on childcare, education and religion, and for a time being were active in the Radical Party's referenda campaigns for divorce, end of hunting, abortion. 'Bagni woman' missed out on the whole feminist thing, consciousness raising, self-examination, etc so the Consultorio, the family planning clinic, with the first vasectomy service in Italy, which I set up and ran in Lucca for the Marie Stopes organisation, was also atypical.

> Now Vincenzo's dead, I seem to have reverted to being a Londoner who spends 6 months a year in Italy. My children and baby grandchild are sooooo Italian. Families are amazing and weird.

I met the poet Mike Rosen soon after I came to live in London when he and I were often protesting about the same things in the heady days of the Inner London Education Authority and the Greater London Council. He often came into William Patten Primary School to entertain the children and supported the school when two of the children were deported, with their parents, to Turkey. I studied at one time with his father Harold who taught me more about language than anyone before or since:

> My mother's parents lived in Hackney and spoke Yiddish. My father's mother lived in Whitechapel, Harold Hill and Barking and spoke Yiddish. My father's father lived

in Brockton and Boston, Massachusetts, and spoke Yiddish and probably some Polish and some German.

My mother understood Yiddish but only used a few words. She learned French at school. My father understood Yiddish and spoke quite a few words and phrases. He was a good speaker of German, which he had learned in the army of occupation in Germany, but aided by his knowledge of Yiddish. He was a good speaker, reader and writer of French, which he learned at school and used many times on holidays and occasionally professionally. He learned Latin at school and university – could read it. He learned Old English at University and taught it and could read it.

I speak English with a smattering of Yiddish words used for fun rather than functionally. I can speak, read and write French, learned at school and on many visits to France and occasional translation jobs. I speak it on holidays.

One of my sons speaks a bit of French learned at school and on holidays; one son speaks quite good Spanish learned at school, subsidiary study at University and used during a gap year. My teenage daughter is studying French and Mandarin and my stepdaughter has an Italian father and her Italian is expanding on visits to Italy, etc.

The next story comes from Anne Sassoon, whom I met on an abstract art course and with whom I share many interests and experiences.

On my father's side: I think my great-grandparents came to Boston from – name kept changing – Poland/Russia. Spoke Yiddish and some English(?). My grandfather was born in Poland/Russia, spoke Yiddish and heavily accented English. He and male relatives knew written Hebrew and ritual Hebrew. My father spoke English and a bit of Yiddish.

On my mother's side: Her parents came to Boston from Lithuania, spoke and read Yiddish and heavily accented English. You had to read aloud anything they wrote in transliterated English in order to make sense of it!

My mother: She was born in the USA, spoke English, knew a little Yiddish, studied Latin and I think French in high school and German as part of a degree but only spoke English.

My father: He too was born in the USA, spoke English, knew some Yiddish and would, I think, have studied Latin and probably French in high school. Only spoke English.

Me: I was born in the USA, speak English and am fluent if imperfect in colloquial Italian. I studied Latin and French in high school and French, Swedish and Italian at university as part of an American-style degree. I learned Swedish when I spent 9 months living with a Swedish-speaking family and going to a Swedish language high school in Helsinki on an exchange programme. Still understand some, particularly in the Swedish-Finnish accent, but fluency has long gone. Although I continued to study French on and off – a record set all those years ago, a brief summer course in France, and from listening to my in-laws (see below) speak it. I have a fair understanding, can read French, but my spoken French is rudimentary to say the least. I learned Italian during an intense 10-week university-level summer course in California and then when I spent a university year in Padua. I moved to London for post-graduate work. I've kept Italian up through frequent visits, a sabbatical term in Italy, Italian academic conferences, Italian friends, and studying Gramsci and other topics in Italian. I studied Spanish on tape when I was visiting our students in Spain. Something has stuck.

My daughter was born in London, spent a term in an Italian school at ages 6 to 7, became fluent in Italian in 6 weeks, did Italian GCSE, still speaks it a bit. Did French GCSE. She was exposed to Italian and French when visiting her paternal grandparents in Italy.

Her paternal grandparents were/are from Egypt. French was their first language. Her paternal grandfather learned English after being drafted into the British Navy during World War II – he had a British passport. Her paternal grandmother learned English in an English-language school in Cairo. They both knew/know some Arabic. They moved to Paris and then Milan after 1948 and learned Italian in Italy.

After reading some of the language histories in this collection, Anne added this:

It was fun to read these language histories. I could add that I use Yiddish expressions the same way that Sandra and Mike do, but then in the US many Yiddish words have entered common usage. Mike and I exchanged emails once about his grandfather and Boston! I can also very much empathise with changes in personality when speaking another language. I sometimes think I blossom in Italian. Native speakers are impressed with my Italian, I think, because of my vivacity and use of colloquialisms – along with mistakes and a variable accent!

The next language history was sent to me by a woman called Rosa Ochoa. I don't know Rosa but she is a friend of my brother's partner, Marisa Mottola. Her account is extremely detailed and she looks back as far as her great grandparents. It will not surprise you to learn that she is an expert in the field of teaching languages and hence knows a great deal about the subject both personally and intellectually.

My grandparents spoke Spanish. My mother's grandparents were from the south of Spain, Jaen (Andalucía) therefore spoke with an Andalusian accent. I never knew my grandfather, as he died when my mother was 16. I knew my grandmother and spent a lot of time with her, either when I visited Jaen from Huesca (where I was born and where I lived) or when she visited us for longish periods of time. Jaen's accent is very different to Castilian as spoken in Aragon. One of the main differences is that they do not pronounce the -s (a plural marker in Spanish), and instead they open up the vowels to mark the plural. As a child, I always ended up with an Andalusian accent, to the merriment of all our Aragonese friends on returning to Huesca. My father's parents were from La Rioja and spoke very good Castilian. Not sure whether I lost my Aragonese accent when I visited them.

My mother spoke with an Andalusian accent and after nearly 60 years living in Aragon, her accent is still noticeable with just saying one word. Nevertheless when she talks to her relatives, they all think she has got an Aragonese accent. I think her intonation may have changed a bit, but not her pronunciation. My father had a very good Spanish (Castilian) accent and very good diction. When they were dating (he was working near Jaen when they met) there were some funny anecdotes and misunderstandings because of different colloquial expressions. This is one of them: my mother told him that that afternoon they would meet and go out with the kids ('los niños'). To my father's surprise, they went out and met a group of young adults their own age. Niños is children in most parts of Spain, but in my mother's circle/town/region it was used to mean their friends.

I was born in Huesca, Aragon. We speak standard Spanish with a sing song accent, but standard pronunciation. There are a few words that are different and I suffered some perplexing misunderstandings when I was a child because of my mother's Andalusian Spanish. For example, I went to school and I said I had forgotten my 'rebeca' at home and was a bit cold. Nobody knew what I meant. All my friends used the word 'chaqueta' for a cardigan, but I had learnt 'rebeca' from my mother. Apparently this term became popular after the 1940 movie *Rebecca* by Alfred Hitchcock, where Joan Fontaine wore twin-sets, hence the term.

I learned French as a child and when I was 11 my parents sent me to a 'Colonie de vacances' near Bordeaux. I don't remember having any problems with the language. I must have already known it quite well. What I remember is that after that summer of immersion, I never had to study much for the rest of my high school years. In fact, the teachers used to tell me and another friend who also knew French to go to the back of the classroom and do other things; otherwise we might spoil it for the rest of the students.

I started learning English at home with a private tutor. When I was at university I decided to do English instead of French, mainly because I could see French was on the decline, but mostly because that meant I had to change to another university, where all my friends were. In spite of knowing the grammar, having quite a wide vocabulary, etc, it was a shock when I spent one year in London as an assistant teacher in Neasden High School. Most of the friends I made were either Irish or Australians … not easy to understand! It took me a while to be confident and start laughing at the right time because I finally got their jokes!

Coming to Australia was another shock to the system. Some of our friends here had very broad accents and didn't enunciate or open their mouths too widely (not to let the flies in, I was told). Now I'm not sure sometimes of the proper pronunciation for certain things (they're, we're, you're is pronounced very differently in Oz …), if I say it like I learnt it, /ðeər/, my husband corrects me and I cannot bring myself to say it like he wants me to. But then again, I haven't totally lost my Spanish accent …

My husband is Italian of Calabrese heritage. His mother would speak to us in Italian and his father and grandmother would speak to us in Calabrese. I love both languages dearly, but do not speak Calabrese well. I went to Italian lessons for a while, but basically I have learnt the language orally and by guessing vocabulary, syntax and grammar from my Spanish. Obviously this doesn't always work, but I can have conversations about nearly anything. My dream is to learn Italian properly when I retire and have time to study it better and hopefully live in Italy for some time.

I worked as an ESL teacher for many years and as an interpreting and translating teacher for the last 5 years (at TAFE, which is a Further Education institution). I have been exposed to many languages, Arabic, Farsi, Mandarin, Japanese, Serbian. … I have had great fun with students and colleagues talking about the pleasures and difficulties of learning a second or third language. Even now dealing with Spanish speaking students from Latin American countries, we wonder at the linguistic richness of Spanish and at how it makes the job of an interpreter quite challenging, but exciting.

I have two sons, Miguel and Gabriel. Miguel was 6 months old when we came to Australia. I spoke to him in Spanish, my husband spoke to him in English and my husband's family spoke to him in Italian and Calabrese. He did Spanish at school and speaks it very well. We have gone back to Spain nearly on a yearly basis, so he was exposed to it all the time. I did a little study of his language learning as part of my Masters in linguistics (code switching) and it was very interesting to see how he knew who to talk to in what language. Never made a mistake and occasionally would code switch within a sentence and use all four languages without making any grammatical errors.

Gabriel was born 5 years later, which means he had Miguel to talk to, and of course they did it in English, not Spanish or Italian. Gabriel was cared for by his grandparents and great grandmother on a daily basis. He did Italian at school and went on an exchange. His Italian was very good, better than his Spanish. But now that his grandparents are dead, he is losing it a bit. Whenever he goes to Spain, he picks

Spanish up quickly, but he is not as good as his older brother. His girlfriend is Swedish and when they visited Sweden last year, he picked up a bit of the language. She has such good English that nobody notices she is not Aussie (tells something about Northern Europe and language teaching!).

I read this language history with amazement. It is such a testament to the ability of human beings to adapt to new languages and cultures, to see patterns and rules and apply them so that learning a new language seems to become easier each time. And, as Rosa says, it tells us such a lot about how bilingualism and multilingualism are the norm in many places, with the Anglo world remaining almost isolated by its dependence on only English.

And here is a tiny language history sent to me by Margaret Tung who now lives in Australia. She told me initially that she speaks both Cantonese and Mandarin and I asked her how she chose which language to use and when. I can almost see the disbelief on her face at the stupidity of my question.

Basically I speak Cantonese to the Cantonese speakers and Mandarin to the Mandarin speakers, whatever it takes to facilitate communication with others. I was taught only Cantonese at home, then when I started going to school I discovered there was another language out there. So I picked up Mandarin in school with some help from my father. When we were very young, the rules at home were that we should speak only Cantonese at home, we were fined if we spoke Mandarin. Also my grandmothers didn't speak Mandarin. I don't think one language is more formal than the other. But these days my Cantonese is only good for conversational use and I wouldn't try to deliver a formal speech in Cantonese, but I can understand others fully.

My own language history is very simple.

I grew up in apartheid South Africa. My parents had both been child immigrants from Eastern Europe: my mother from Latvia and my father from Russia. My maternal grandparents were educated and spoke German, Russian and Yiddish. Both were literate. They had three children. My oldest aunt, Gessy, was taught initially by a governess but went to secondary school where she had some teaching in Lettish or Latvian, which was the official language, but which my mother calls the language of the privileged. My paternal grandparents were little educated, although my grandfather was a teacher of Hebrew which suggests that he must have been literate too. I know that they spoke Yiddish at home but do not know if they spoke Russian and/or German as well.

When both sets fled the pogroms in Europe they went to South Africa, one lot with three children and the other lot with seven. So almost all of my parents' generation had first languages that they soon lost as they were required to learn both English and Afrikaans – the two official languages in the country at that time – in their new homes. The only one to retain Russian was Gessy who was 16 when they went to South Africa. She later became a lecturer in Russian here in the UK. Apartheid South Africa had two official or dominant languages – English and Afrikaans. The languages of the majority of the people of the country – the black people – were totally disregarded. You will almost certainly know that after the end of apartheid the new government decided that the country should have 11 official languages. These include English and Afrikaans, which now have the same status as the nine African languages.

So I had to learn Afrikaans and chose to learn French at school. When I went on holiday to France in my early twenties, lines of French poetry came into my head as I recited aloud the names of all the French adverts and signs we passed. Later I learned Italian on the hoof initially and then by going on conversation classes in London and in Italy. I get by in Italian and love it when it works, but I classify myself as monolingual. A deep regret in my life is that I did not learn other languages.

Of my generation of my extended family almost all have left South Africa. Many of us are monolinguals in the UK or USA. One or two have learned Hebrew. One of my daughters is bilingual Russian/English and three grandchildren in Australia learn Hebrew. We have lost Yiddish – although I understand some and use some phrases, like Mike Rosen and Anne Sassoon, for fun and emphasis – and almost lost Russian and German. But on my first visit to Berlin I found myself able to understand some German and attribute that to its similarity to Yiddish.

When I went back to live and work in South Africa some years ago I decided to try to learn isiZulu, and attended a weekly class. The teacher would not allow me to write anything down, telling me that we learn languages through our ears. When I argued that I had had a lifetime of writing things down as part of attempts to remember and felt adrift without access to this, she just laughed. At the end of the course I felt that I had not learned one word of isiZulu.

When I was in South Africa I became friends with Snoeks Desmond, who lives and works with young children in Durban. In her language history she says this about trying to learn Zulu.

> I tried many different ways of learning Zulu – tapes, a computer program, talking to colleagues – but never made much headway although I really did want to. I just couldn't remember much.

I wonder if this is anything to do with trying to learn a non-European language or trying to learn a new language when past middle age.

What we learn from this

You will almost certainly have recognised that many of those contributing their language histories are now privileged people as a result, often, of having had to move and then being able to benefit from education, gain reasonably paid work and sustain a more middle-class lifestyle alone or with their families. Think of Janos leaving school at 14; of my grandfather similarly leaving school at more or less the same age.

So almost all are people coming from poor families, often forced to move, and now essentially middle aged or older people, professional, middle class and living in the developed world. For many, their grandparents and/or parents had lived in poverty or faced discrimination and many acquired their new languages and sometimes lost their own languages through emigration – which is the situation currently facing millions of young children today.

My analysis of what we can learn from these language histories is this:

- Where people are forced to move from one country to another they often face having to learn a new language (L2), and in the process and over time may often *lose their first language* (L1). With the loss of your first language you lose your culture and your close ties to your extended family.
- Some bilingual children are made to feel embarrassed or ashamed of having more than one language and in some situations refuse to use this or these language/s and sometimes invent solutions to hide their language abilities. The issues of *belonging or being seen as an outsider and being judged as different* underpin some of the stories. You get clear evidence of this in the case of Raymonde hiding her skills by deliberately making mistakes.
- Some adults *stop using their first language with their children for fear that it will stop them progressing in their second language*. There is much evidence of this in the new South Africa where, despite a policy of cultural celebration, many parents want their children to be taught in English, which is seen as being a more worthwhile and respected language. There is evidence in some of the stories that some, in later life, regret this lost opportunity. Others stop because the children become resistant. This is evident in the language history of Hong-Bich.
- By contrast, some parents or grandparents make a *conscious decision to ensure that their first language is spoken to children and grandchildren*. Usually the reason is to ensure that the language and culture and the links to grandparents and extended family members are retained. Several histories reveal this – Marion's and Rosa's, for example.
- Some children of bilingual parents *refuse to speak the first language of the parents*. They may fear being teased or ridiculed or being called stupid. This is evident in the story of Hong-Bich.

- Some people *speak their first language at home and with family and the second language away from home and with others.*
- Some regard the acquisition of *other languages as something wonderful* – offering the possibility of adopting a different personality, being admitted to other worlds, or as a passport into different cultures and ideas. This was evident in the stories of Marion and Carol and you will find more later in the book.
- Issues of class or gender or race emerge as people talk about *accents* – often negatively – or about using a particular language with particular groups of people – as in the case of speaking Portuguese with the servants! Carol's history, again, illustrates this.
- *Learning a new language seems very easy for young children.* This may be an illusion, as we will see later in the book. But there is evidence that once you have learned more than one language each new language gets easier to learn.
- There are some illustrations of how *the knowledge of one language can assist in the learning of another* – as in the case of Yiddish and German. There is also a recognition of just how speakers of more than one language use their linguistic knowledge to find similarities with other languages.
- In many of the case studies *different ways of learning language are cited* – for example using recordings, formal learning at school or university, on holiday, through living with others.

I end this chapter with an extract from a poem called *My language and I* by Theodor Kallifatides:

> I have lost my language
> things have no taste any more
> in my mouth
> there is always an infinite
> silent moment
> between me and the new words ...
> (in Skutnabb-Kangas & Cummins, 1988: 167)

Chapter 2

Being bilingual

The year 1978 was the one in which I came to live and work in London and also the year when the *Bilingual Under Fives Project* (often referred to as BUF), run by the Inner London Education Authority (ILEA), started. The project was dear to my heart because, having come from apartheid South Africa via Manchester, where I qualified as a teacher, I had a developing interest in how to offer appropriate opportunities for the growing numbers of young children with languages other than English entering our schools and settings. It was in the work of Pauline France and Trish Green (1978), teacher tutors at the Centre for Urban Educational Studies (CUES), that I first encountered people actually working with bilingual nursery children and ensuring that these children learned a second language (English) and, more importantly, were actively encouraged to maintain their first languages whilst doing this. France and Green's accounts of what they and colleagues were doing were published in the early 1980s and these showed just how intent they were on recognising and exploring bilingualism as an advantage and not as a barrier to learning and succeeding academically. For example, influenced by Sylvaine Wiles (who was also deeply involved in the field but primarily with secondary school pupils) they used the word bilingual in preference to the more negative terms common at the time – such as second language learner, ESL learner, non-English speaker and, most alarmingly, non-speaker. Here is Wiles's definition:

> The bilingual child is one who is learning and using two languages (one of which is the Mother tongue) irrespective of levels of achievement in the languages at any point in time. This may seem too inclusive a category. It certainly lacks precision, but bilingualism is a very complex phenomena and precision in this area may well be unattainable.
>
> (Wiles, 1979: 284, now out of print)

Accompanying the work of BUF and other organisations within the ILEA, the debate began in schools and settings about how children born out of the

UK, from different belief systems and speaking languages other than English, could possibly succeed in our educational system. Bilingual children were still considered to have no language and hence no experience of any value. Such negative and deficit views of these children clashed with what many educationalists were learning about child development through reading the words of such writers and thinkers as Lev Vygotsky, Jerome Bruner, Paolo Freire, Susan Isaacs and others. They were all talking of children as active learners, problem solvers, question askers and meaning makers.

In the 1970s I was working in an infant school in inner-city Hackney. At that school, like many other schools across the country, there were nearly 70 languages spoken by the pupils and their families. The main *second language* was Turkish, and other languages included Gujarati, Bengali, Punjabi, Greek, Spanish, Hindi, Urdu, Arabic, Cantonese, Vietnamese and more. All of us working in the school came to see this rich linguistic diversity as an asset. What opportunities this offered us, the teachers, to learn more about language per se. The number of languages in schools and settings across the country has increased since then: bilingualism or multilingualism is becoming the norm in our urban centres and even in some rural settings. And this is true of almost all cities in the world. Wars, poverty, climate change, discrimination, religious and ethnic division and the lure of 'better' things have all caused huge numbers of people to choose or be forced to seek lives in other places. In one sense England, having English as its *majority language*, has not paid much attention to the value of bilingualism, believing that everyone speaks or would like to speak English. As a consequence of this we are still a country where the learning and speaking of other languages is not valued. My own grandchildren left or will leave school having learned a minimal amount of one European language. Because of our colonial role throughout the world we were able to expect others to learn our language rather than recognising the benefits of learning and speaking other languages.

Jim Cummins, one of the most respected researchers and writers on bilingualism, considered the issue of globalisation and its impact on schools and settings. He noted that, as more and more people were forced into or chose to leave their countries in search of work or liberty or equality or a decent life, so the cultural, linguistic, racial and religious make up of countries around the world changed. Alongside this the places of learning – schools and setting, colleges and universities – found themselves dealing with large groups of people whose needs had never before been adequately addressed. Some people welcomed this new diversity but there were concerns about how best to deal with the issues raised. And in some countries there was strong opposition from neo-fascist groups to these new-comers who were seen as foreigners and scroungers. There were, of course, also those who were more tolerant and urged assimilation, but very often this meant the newcomers having to adapt to the culture, language and conventions of the host country. Scant recognition was given to the things the newcomers brought with them in terms of culture and customs that might enhance their new countries. In many countries there were those arguing for excluding immigrants or keeping them in separate schools and settings and others advising their assimilation into existing provision. Cummins said:

> 'assimilation' is similar in many ways to 'exclusion' insofar as both orientations are designed to make the 'problem' disappear.... Assimilationist policies in education discourage students from maintaining their mother tongues. If students retain their culture and language, then they are viewed as less capable of identifying with the mainstream culture and learning the mainstream language of the society.
>
> (2001: 15)

In both cases the incomers were seen as a problem needing to be solved. Those who want to keep their mother tongue are urged to give it up if they want to be truly accepted in the school and society. This, as you can imagine, can have terrible implications for children and their families.

> It violates children's right to an appropriate education and undermines communication between children and their parents. Any credible educator will agree that schools should build on the experience and knowledge that children bring to the classroom, and instruction should also promote children's abilities and talents. Whether we do it intentionally or inadvertently, when we destroy children's language and rupture their relationship with parents and grandparents, we are contradicting the very essence of education.
>
> (Cummins, 2001:15–16)

The challenge then for us – the educators and policy-makers – is to try to begin to build a common identity for our citizens which is truly respectful of all that every child brings in terms of language, family structure, culture, experience and values so that children themselves are perceived as having real rights as contributors to creating a complex national or universal identity that continues to change and develop. We should not squander the rich linguistic resources newcomers bring with them.

How, then, can schools provide an appropriate education for culturally and linguistically diverse children? A first step is to learn what the research says about the role of language, and specifically children's mother tongues, in their educational development. This is a running theme throughout this book.

You might think that learning English or any other second or subsequent language is simple for very young children who are immersed in it in a classroom or setting. Alongside other children of their age, hearing them talk to one another, sitting beside them as they draw and paint, listening to the songs they sing and noticing the patterns of the new language, seems like the ideal way of learning a language. The reality, however, is different and darker.

Fatih Hasbudak – who now likes to be called Flint – sent me his moving language history, which you can read below. He and his sister Zeynep became pupils at William Patten Primary School after their parents, of Turkish origin, came to the UK as economic migrants. Theirs was a united small family, living an everyday life, when they were suddenly faced with deportation on the spurious grounds of being 'overstayers'. The Home Office of the then Thatcher government told the parents that their two children, Zeynep, aged 7, and Fatih, aged 5, could remain in the UK because they had been born here. Because there were no relatives to care for the children the government would pay for them to be put in the care of the local authority. Both children were, by then, bilingual. William Patten Primary School led a very public and passionate appeal against this and little Zeynep became the spokesperson for the whole family. She spoke for herself, her little brother and her parents whose English was rudimentary. She spoke at rallies and interviews on television. The family went into hiding until Polak, the father, was lured out to collect a parcel from the post office where he was arrested and within 24 hours deported in the clothes he stood up in. The campaign had failed, despite massive support from parents, teachers, other schools, trades unionists and others and soon afterwards the whole family left for Istanbul. Many years later I found both children – no longer children – here in London. And when I met them Zeynep – that fluent and articulate English speaker – had completely lost her English and was here on a language course, trying to regain it. Trauma had silenced her and made her lose her English voice. But here is Fatih/Flint's voice:

> My father's parents migrated to Turkey in the 1920s from around the Caspian Sea, southern Russia. They and their extended family spoke the Avar language, if I'm not mistaken with the name. I've never met them, but I'm led to believe they were also native or became like native-speakers in the Turkish language over the years. My mother's parents were from a north eastern city of Turkey called Trabzon. They both were native Turkish speakers but their background may go a different route if looked deeper. Both my parents are monolingual: they speak Turkish at home and were schooled in the Turkish language.

> I speak predominantly English nowadays but still in Turkish with my sister when we're alone, and Turkish with my parents. I don't have any children, but my sister speaks Turkish with my nieces (she gave birth to her second daughter last Thursday). I speak with them in Turkish most of the time but also in English if there are non-Turkish speakers around.

> Perhaps one of the most interesting things about both the languages I speak is that I feel the need to use a language specific name for each language. I don't remember

if we spoke about this earlier, but I legally adopted the name Flint many years ago, which made my life a lot easier in social terms compared to the use of a Turkish name Fatih here in England. That approach also affected and preserved my bilingual and bicultural abilities in many other ways. What I mean by that is, I believe a person's name can sometimes define identity and culture and therefore requires a little more cultural and linguistic awareness on both nationalities if I am to possess two. Plus I'd refuse to have any name denoting any sort of religion or nationalism. These points and the way Fatih is pronounced in English made me feel to choose an additional one.

An interesting study about what is known as a *third space* was carried out by Julia López-Robertson and Susan Schramm-Pate (2013), who examined what happened when a 6-year-old child was invited to use her bilingualism in school. The child, given the name of Gabriela for the purposes of the research paper, was a pupil at an elementary school in the United States. She was a speaker of both English and Spanish and she and her fellow pupils were fortunate to have a socially conscious and perceptive teacher, given the name of Mrs Perez, who knew enough about the pupils and their homes and families to attempt to ask them to start to reveal aspects of their home or out-of-school experience in the classroom. This teacher knew, as all good educators do, that a respectful knowledge of the languages, customs, cultures and experience of her pupils was essential not only to their successful learning but also to her successful teaching. Mrs Perez announced that the class was going to study migrant farm workers as their term project. This in itself is an interesting and unusual project, suggesting much about the teacher herself. The children would have opportunities to listen to guest speakers, watch video documentaries and read some books in both English and Spanish and – perhaps most significantly – take these home. While this was being spelled out to the class Gabriela was doodling on her notebook cover, half paying attention, but when she heard about being able to take the books home she:

> stopped doodling and looked up with bright eyes when she heard her teacher say that the class was not only going to discuss the presentations and books just in Spanish but tell stories about their families too! She whispered audibly to herself, 'en Espanol!', as she began to happily squirm and fidget in her chair.
>
> (López-Robertson & Schramm-Pate, 2013: 41)

Gabriela interpreted this as an invitation not only to speak Spanish but also to tell the true stories about her own family. The school had classified Gabriela as what they called an '*emerging bilingual*' student, by which they meant that her language abilities were far stronger in her first language, Spanish, than in her school language. And although she was able to work successfully in academic

English in the classroom and understand what was said, only occasionally having to search for a word, she preferred her first language of Spanish. She said:

> 'El ingles no me viene' which, loosely translated means English doesn't come to me, implying it is not natural. Gabriela has very strong opinions regarding the use of Spanish in school, opinions she is not afraid to share. Even as a young girl, she believes children should be allowed to use Spanish in school as freely as they use English.
>
> (López-Robertson & Schramm-Pate, 2013: 41)

López-Robertson and Schramm-Pate chose to analyse this episode in an interesting way by carrying out what they called 'a *hybridity analysis*', using a conceptual framework developed by Bhabha (1994) where the 'in-between spaces' can carry out the role of making meaning of culture, curriculum and collaboration. In any classroom or setting there will be the *mainstream culture* and its associated L1 or mother tongue books, and a *secondary culture* with its L2 or second language books and also a *third* or *hybrid space* where a child like Gabriela can become an insider and the holder of knowledge and culture. So in this example, where the first language is English and the second Spanish, a Spanish speaking child can become the expert, as we see with what happened to Gabriela. She was enabled to delve into the hybrid or 'third space' (which you will remember is the in-between space between her home life and her classroom life) and it was her actions in this space that focused this qualitative research. Qualitative research is used primarily to gain an understanding of underlying reasons, opinions and motivations.

This paper, although a little dated, is an important and carefully argued political analysis. In summary it suggests that the third or hybrid space is where children who have been silenced or marginalised in some way can bring their own stories and life experiences into the class or setting. In other words it can be seen as the bridge between the more formal script and language of the classroom and the personal scripts of those whose languages and cultures are not those of the mainstream. It offers children the possibility to question, to offer an alternative version, or to not only become part of the mainstream dialogue but be able to take charge of it for a while.

Being bilingual can mean being silenced or marginalised. We have talked of the silent period and those of you familiar with the work of Paolo Freire, who spent his long life addressing issues related to why so many people are silenced or othered, will link this analysis to his work. It is evident that those who become silenced may be those who have experienced struggle in their lives. They may have had to move country, change language, face being outsiders and newcomers, dealt with discrimination. To counter this in young children we need to invite, recognise and celebrate what they bring to the culture of the class and setting. Just as Gabriela does. Here is how she made very personal links from her own life and culture to the story of *Tomas the Library Lady* (in Spanish):

> She pointed to the part in the book where Tomas was seen sleeping on a cot and told the story of her own family long ago. She began as she did most of her stories with '*Esta pagina me recordo cuando*' (which means, 'This page reminds me …') and continued '*vivíamos en Atil, porque dormíamos en camitas así y dormíamos en, en como casí, eso de, casi como "tents", pero no son "tents", son casitas así que*' (which means 'This page reminded me when we lived in Atil, because we used to sleep in beds like this and we slept in, in, kind of like, this, almost like tents, but not tents, little houses'). She went on to tell the class that her father, a migrant worker, came home tired and with a bad back from all the bending and lifting.
>
> (López-Robertson & Schramm-Pate, 2013: based on 49)

Within the third space, created in this case by the teacher, emerging bilingual students like Gabriela can share their particular experience and expertise about something relating to their real lives. They become the holders of knowledge. Those working with young children need to remember to always consider the importance of knowing about and respecting the home lives of their pupils in all their aspects. Good early years practitioners already know that it is essential to allow children to draw on their previous experience gained from their everyday life experiences. Where a child – any child – has a space where what she knows and has experienced can be shared with others, she will reveal the extent of her ability to raise and solve problems, remember, describe and contribute. If this interests you, you will find many wonderful examples of bilingual children teaching one another about their cultures and languages in the work of Charmian Kenner (e.g. 2004a, b).

Rosa Ochoa's little boys (cited earlier) were bilingual in a community where that was the norm. They were able to enjoy talking to people from all the layers of their lives – parents, friends, grandparents, one another, at school, at home. When I went back to South Africa in 1996 and worked on a national early childhood project, the three young members of my team – none of them from advantaged backgrounds – could speak, read and write all 11 official languages. Within their communities this multilingualism was the norm. My monolingualism stunned them.

Bilingual children grow up with more than one language in different contexts. Cleo, whose language history appears later in this book, grew up in an Italian village, with English and Italian, where Italian was the majority language. But both languages were regarded as important and worth having. Romero (son of a neighbour of mine) grew up in Mozambique and his father spoke Portuguese and his mother Shimakonde. In Mozambique Portuguese was far more highly valued than the African language spoken by Romero's mother. Much then depends on the value placed by society on the languages in question. Children speaking two European languages are celebrated as being 'clever'; those speaking possibly three Asian languages are generally not.

The task facing any bilingual infant seems daunting. Yet millions of children acquire and use two or more languages. This is how Macrory (2006) explains the complexities facing the child. The bilingual child has to learn two different phonological or sound systems, where there may be phonemes present in one language but not in the other. The phoneme is a perceptually distinct unit of sound in that it distinguishes one word from another, for example p, b, d and t in the English words pad, pat, bad and bat. Even more complex, perhaps, there may be phonemic distinctions that are meaningful in one language but not in the other; there may be differences in stress and intonation. In the area of *syntax* (the way words are ordered to make a sentence, for example) and *morphology* (the morpheme is the smallest meaning-bearing unit of language and morphology is the study of the internal structure of words) numerous differences are possible such as word order, the use (or not) of pronouns with verbs, the construction of tenses and other grammatical and morphological differences. Pragmatically, there are differences in rules governing politeness, register and so on (based on Macrory, 2006: 162–163).

And beyond that the child has to learn to function as a bilingual – which implies learning the rules governing code-switching (now called translanguage) from one language to another in order to function in her bilingual community.

Jane Miller, writing in 1983, defined a bilingual person as '*someone who operates during their everyday life in more than one language and does so with some degree of self-confidence*' (Miller, 1983: x) – a very straightforward definition. Many years later, Carol Myers-Scotton (2005: 44) defined bilingualism as '*the ability to use two or more languages sufficiently to carry out limited casual conversations*' and Leung *et al.* (1997) speak of *language expertise, language affiliation* and *language inheritance*, all of which form a person's *language identity*. Some theorists talk about the *one person/one language* strategy, which certain childcare experts feel is successful and tend to recommend to parents. What it means is that the parent who speaks Italian, for example, should always use Italian while the parent who speaks English should always use English with the child. But can we really describe this as being one person one language? Surely the child hears the parents speak to one another in either or both the languages. Once the parents speak to each other, one of them – by definition – must switch language, so that children must, for some of the time, be exposed to translanguage. In some cases one parent may have reached a higher level of education and hence perhaps uses more complex linguistic forms, or one parent may associate one language with negative experiences. Jill Lane, first encountered on a painting holiday in France, said of her complex and involved language history:

> My mother Joan was born in London and spoke English. She spent a year in Belgium to refine her French and music and became a fluent French speaker and learned some Pushtu. My father Ralph was born in Pakistan, was fluent in both Pushtu and English and had spent time in Paris before the war to increase his French. Was seen to translate his French into Pushtu! As a primary teacher he would take the Devon children to task in Pushtu when they were becoming disruptive in class and achieved silence they had never heard the like. I was born in England and spent time in both Malaya and Afghanistan, learned French and German at school. Our home language was scattered with Pushtu and other words which seemed normal to us. We were surprised to learn that other people didn't know what was meant.

How interesting that, for Jill, hearing and using Pushtu words in English sentences was normal and it was a surprise that not everyone did the same thing.

The experiences of being bilingual are varied. Some bilingual children will produce *mixed utterances*, using both languages in one sentence. But monolingual children do something similar when they invent words, as my younger daughter did when she looked at me across the table and said '*I am oppositting you*'. (Not surprisingly the spellcheck on this computer does not like this word!) The notion that a young child suffers cognitive confusion by being exposed to more than one language is both outdated and incorrect. So is the earlier idea that bilingual children operate with a single system, suggesting that they are not aware of having two languages. There is increasing evidence that, far from being confused or unaware, young children are able to differentiate between the two languages in their environment from an early age. They know which language to speak to which person and in what contexts. Young bilingual children develop and use two separate linguistic systems from early on in grammatical development. Research shows that infants recognise the voices of key people from soon after birth, and pay special attention to someone speaking a language that is not that of the mother (Mehler *et al.*, 1988) and are able to detect the differences between their two languages before 5 months of age, despite any similarities that exist between the sound systems of the two languages (Bosch & Sebastian-Galles, 2001). Many children learn a second or other language after having learned their first or mother tongue. We see this in our schools and settings where many young children arrive with one or more languages learned in the home and then start to acquire the new language of English. By the time the children arrive at your school or setting they have already learned their first language or languages and it is important to always remember that learning starts before birth, then in the home, so by the time you meet the child she already has her own language history.

As Vygotsky (1978: 84) said, '*Children's learning begins long before they attend school so any learning encountered in school by a child has a previous history*'.

Children learning their first language/s in the home are immersed in the language, which is always contextualised. It relates to the people and events within the everyday life of the family. It is both verbal and non-verbal and is repetitive in the sense of happening around the ordinary real-life events of the home – eating, playing, sleeping, story times, going for walks, relating to family members, bath time and more. It is meaningful and purposeful, rooted in the social interactions within the home and community. When the child arrives in the classroom or setting and encounters the new language on a daily basis it is in a completely different learning environment. Gone is the dialogic relationship and intimacy of language use in the home. Here the adults tend to dominate in conversation as shown in many studies, going as far back as that of Gordon Wells (1986): '*As repeatedly emphasized, conversation is a reciprocal activity; the more one participant dominates, the more opportunities for the other participant to make his or her own personal contribution are reduced and constrained*' (1986: 87).

In classrooms and settings you often hear things said over and over again as the adult asks questions and children answer. This is reciprocal, but in many cases it is the adult who controls and dominates, making it less possible for the young bilingual child to be drawn in.

What we learn from this

We learn that the young bilingual child has an enormous cognitive and social task to accomplish in learning to communicate using more than one language. Those working with young bilingual children need to remain sensitive to what it is the child is attempting to communicate and respectful of the languages and cultures involved.

Chapter 3

How language can define you

When I asked people to tell me about their languages, I did not ask about accent or dialect. So it surprised me that so many of those who responded talked about both of these issues. Often the comment was pejorative – things like 'execrable' or 'broad' or 'sing-song' or 'city' or 'heavily accented' and often with regard to someone speaking English. When I first came to England, with English as my first language but spoken with a South African accent, people couldn't place me in terms of class. I did not speak like those who had been to Eton but nor did I speak like someone born within the sound of Bow bells. When I lived in Manchester it took me several years to understand the jokes told in our local pub. My language 'othered' me in this small way.

This was my introduction to the clearly defined class system in the UK together with its links to language(s) and accent. There was no comparable class system in apartheid South Africa because discrimination was built into the racist system of the country. Here in the UK it was perfectly acceptable to speak a European language like French and to have learned some Latin and Greek. But was it really true that there were languages named Lettish, Aragonese and KiSwahili and who, if anybody, still spoke Yiddish? There exists a veritable hierarchy of languages. This discrimination – judging a person by how she sounds – is more subtle than that of colour or religion or gender but just as insidious. Some years back a researcher played the voices of English speakers to people whose first language was not English and they selected the Birmingham accent as the most pleasant to listen to. For local English speakers the accent of Birmingham is often described as the worst one to listen to.

Mozambique is a country on the south-east coast of Africa. It has had a troubled history dominated by the impact of colonialism. Examining some aspects of its history gives us an illuminating tale of the power and potency of language. The first inhabitants were San hunter-gatherers who were the ancestors of the Khoisani people. For generations, between the first and fourth centuries AD many people spoke the languages of the black people – the so-called 'Bantu' languages, which included both Swahili and Shona that are still prominent and living languages today. Arab trading posts were set up on the coast and nearby islands and in 1498 Vasco da Gama and his troupe of Portuguese explorers reached the area and Mozambique fell under Portuguese rule. There were the African languages of the local people, the languages of the Arab traders and Portuguese. When after World War II many colonial powers were offering their colonies independence Portugal held fast to hers. As a result a coalition of powerful and angry anti-colonial groups called FRELIMO (which stands for Freedom for the Liberation of Mozambique) fought an armed campaign against the Portuguese settlers in 1964. After 10 years of brutal warfare the country gained its independence. A tragic civil war followed during which millions died or sought asylum in neighbouring countries and peace was only restored in 1992. You can imagine what an enormous and daunting task it was to heal and unite this disparate, poorly educated, largely illiterate and very poor people. There were something like 43 different languages spoken but Portuguese remained the official language until arguments began about the fairness of this. Being the official language meant that it was the language of schooling despite not being the language of millions of the people. Discussion began about whether to introduce a programme of bilingual education in the early years, using Portuguese and the heritage languages of the children (based on Kitoko-Nsiku, 2007). There is no space here to detail all the problems facing the country in implementing this programme but the fact that the paper I am citing is called *Dogs' Languages or People's Languages?* tells you all you need to know. Kitoko-Nsiku says:

> The challenge faced by the government, teachers, parents and students during the implementation of this new educational system in primary schools includes revitalisation of Bantu languages and the need to address issues of cultural identity among speakers of languages previously thought of as only fit for dogs.
>
> (2007: 258)

What cultural history can you be expected to have as a speaker of a language fit only for dogs?

One of the questions asked of the participants in my language history study was about the languages spoken by their children, if any. Inevitably, for those emigrating, the loss of a first language is a possibility and often, where the official language of the host country is one as prevalent and dominant as English – think about the Internet and social media – this is a very real possibility. Parents know that learning the host language is essential to success in the future and so they support their children's learning of the new language, sometimes at the expense of the home language. In social and cultural terms this is a serious loss. The child loses the ability to maintain contact with grandparents or other family members and possibly also an interest in the songs and games and stories of this first culture.

Veronica Pacini–Ketchabaw and Ana–Elisa Armstrong de Almeida (2006) carried out an interesting study in Canada, which has two official European languages, English and French, but is also host to many migrants speaking a range of other languages. Both of these official languages are regarded throughout the world as high status languages. The researchers were looking at how the stated good intentions of Canadian education policy makers influenced the decisions made and the consequences these had on the identities of the preschool children and their families. The study in question focused primarily on young children from immigrant families who were attending childcare centres linked to the educational system since one of the roles of childcare centres is to prepare children for school. In British Columbia, where the study was conducted, parents were offered pamphlets about the centres, all written in English, and this was regarded as giving the parents easily accessible information about how to prepare their young children for school. But in addition to them only being written in English, there was much in the pamphlets that emphasised negatives and caused the parents great anxiety. In many countries there are discussions about what is termed school readiness and, in the case of young children having to fit into a culture that is essentially not theirs, anxieties are multiplied.

> Although the discourse of school readiness does not necessarily relate to language issues, language issues are very much implicated and implicit. For example, statements on literacy tend to silence immigrant children (Pacini-Ketchabaw et al., 2006). The overall implicit message about children is 'to overcome the racial [and linguistic] differences ... by diluting them, by bleaching them out through assimilation or integration' (Goldberg, 1993: 7). In the pamphlets, it is assumed: (a) that young children and families are culturally, racially, as well as linguistically homogeneous; (b) that child development theories that emphasise universal aspects of development and child-centred activities are the best for all children regardless of background and abilities; (c) that all children are monolingual, normalising English as the most relevant way to communication for children (Pacini-Ketchabaw et al., 2005). This discourse of cultural, linguistic and racial homogeneity positions children in immigrant families as incomplete human beings, at the beginning of a process of assimilation and, consequently, as having incomplete citizenship status.
>
> (Pacini-Ketchabaw & Armstrong de Almeida, 2006: 310)

This is a serious piece of research and the findings listed above are themes that run through this book. It is worth reading this again.

To support their arguments, the researchers quote some of the comments of the parents of the young children and these, offered below, are powerful reminders of the dangers of tacitly supporting the loss of first languages in early childhood.

> From the beginning they got new friends who speak English, they communicate with each other then when they come home they use English and they can't use Albanian anymore . . . we don't know how much they understand Albanian language anymore. . . . Only English. (Father, Albanian language group, individual interview, Family 20).

> Teachers send you homework in English. You need to read to them [children] in English to help them develop these skills. So I help her with her homework in English. Then, you do not have the time to read or learn your home language. There is no time to really maintain the language. (Mother, Spanish Focus Group, Family 54).

> It is the availability. . . . All the TV programmes and movies and Barney (the dinosaur) other stuff are in English. All the comedies and cartoons, it is very interesting, and this is good for the children to learn English. They quickly understand; it is better than if we try to teach them. The children are quick recipients of learning things, so they learn easily from the television. I guess that was the reason why we said we didn't make a conscious decision; the decision [to stop speaking Tigrigna] was made by society. And this is my assumption and my hypothesis. The decision was made by society. (Mother, Tigrigna Language Group, individual interview, Family 34).
> (Pacini-Ketchabaw & Armstrong de Almeida, 2006: 319–320)

I wonder if you find the words '*the decision for the child to lose her first language was made by society*' chilling.

Cleo Ganz is the daughter of Marion Iacopucci (whose language history appeared earlier in the book). She has lived in both Italy and Germany and spent considerable periods of time in England. She sent me her language history and it is an extremely reflective, personal and sensitive analysis of how her linguistic abilities have affected all aspects of her life and, essentially, her identity. You will notice some of it is in bold text. This is my personal response to some of Cleo's wise or startling or poignant comments.

> My mother's father: German/English. My mother's mother: English, understood German.

> My father Vincenzo was Italian and only spoke Italian, refused to speak or understand English saying he wasn't good at languages. This is rather curious as my mother only spoke English to me and Dario as children. Our grandparents moved to Italy from Lanzarote to stay next door to us when I was around 3 years old. They did not speak Italian and never really learned to. Dario and I were a **speaking link**

between the family. My father was nearly 50 years old when I was born and certainly a different generation from my friends' parents and used (when he wasn't being very Tuscan and involved in excited conversations with colourful blasphemous words) **a beautiful clear Italian, unusually full of detail and meaning**.

I was told lately by Italian friends that they always liked the way I expressed myself because it was different. I owe that to my father. I very much regret not being able to express myself like that anymore, **I'm missing the practice and the lightness and spirit of the language**. . . . So, Vincenzo very cleverly never learned English and very politely maintained his independent world that was always full of English speaking friends and family.

My mother Marion always spoke and read to us in English. As my father did not speak any English we would often have conversations at meal times in two different languages.

The language we spoke and who we spoke to made a big difference to me not only from the language point of view. We were brought up in a small village in Tuscany where traditions, religion and small-minded bigoted people still had a strong influence in people's lives. I was brought up an atheist and wasn't baptised. I was taught to have my own opinion and pursue it. I always felt different, which was hard when I was a kid and desperately wanted to fit in. I always felt special and very different from all my friends. **I eventually luckily knew that I was very privileged and had a freedom in life that not many of my friends would ever feel they had or enjoyed.**

So speaking a different language also meant to me that **I was confronting a completely different culture and I was very soon aware and careful of what I was thinking and able to express in different situations.** I think it might have been more complicated for me as child than for Dario as boys are generally doted on . . . and keep the family name! I fitted in well but never completely in Italy. My friends always felt me as being different and not typically Italian. I never met the expectations of the Italian part of my family except for my father's, I hope. I have always felt Italian rather than English. I suppose it's because I lived in Italy most of my life. I spent at least a month or more in London every year visiting my lovely family with my mother and brother. I went to school in London for a term when I was 11 and had no language problem. I had 3 years of very poor teaching in French, 3 years of Latin and Greek and 2 years of Spanish at school. Don't remember any of it! I started learning German at the age of 19 and didn't really start to speak it until I was about 23. I studied languages (German and English) at an Italian university for 3 years but didn't complete my course of studies. I ended up in Munich to prepare for a German exam and have lived in different parts of Germany ever since. I eventually learned good German taking courses and mainly when my husband just refused to speak English with me anymore. I can make myself understood in English but I'm poor in spelling and definitely not as fluent as I used to be! I don't seem to have strong accents in any language but I'm lacking practice in both English and Italian. **The language I felt most comfortable in was Italian and now I find that in everyday life German is easier but not necessarily better especially if I have to describe what I'm feeling. . . . I feel a bit messed up just trying to think in which language it's really me speaking** . . . does this make sense?

We will all respond very differently to this but what emerges for me – a sad monolingual – is the amazing benefits of knowing languages that Cleo herself recognises. She has thought back with such clarity revealed in passages like: *'My father was nearly 50 years old when I was born and certainly a different generation from my friends' parents and used (when he wasn't being very Tuscan and involved in excited conversations with colourful blasphemous words) a beautiful clear Italian, unusually full of detail and meaning.'* I cannot imagine describing the way someone speaks a language with the clarity that Cleo displays in this extract. Is that because, being monolingual, I pay less attention to the ways in which people speak my only language? She also analysed the roles she and her brother played as translators for their grandparents, describing them as a *'speaking link'*. I have known Cleo for a very long time but it was only through her responding to my questions that I came to see how she used the topic of language to explore so many aspects of her life. The limits of my language are truly the limits of my world!

What we learn from this

Language, which is so closely tied up with culture and links to our past and our heritage, is clearly a defining feature of our lives. We may be judged by the language or languages we speak, the ways in which we speak them, our success in life.

Chapter 4

How we acquire our first and subsequent languages

Language acquisition is a fascinating, tendentious and complex subject and theorists who disagree with one another do so with a passion. The notion that children acquire language largely through imitation dates back to the work of Skinner, who believed that much of language acquisition came about through two processes – imitation and reinforcement. He argued that the child makes a sound; the adult interprets the sound as meaningful and praises the child; the child repeats the sound. Put crudely the model looks like this:

- The child babbles and within the string of sounds comes something that sounds like 'mama' or 'mummy' or 'meme'.
- The mother thinks the child has learned to say the word for mother and kisses the child.

The praise or positive reinforcement – hoping for a kiss or hug in this case – is what makes the child say the word again. The child has learned to say 'mama'. This is a gross oversimplification and it is clear that imitation plays a vital role in the acquisition of language. We will come to this later in this chapter.

Using language in order to communicate is a milestone in development. What is fascinating is that this remarkable intellectual feat, which usually takes place within the first year of life, occurs without anyone giving the child lessons. No one sets out to teach the child to talk. Rather, children begin to communicate with other beings through a range of modalities such as gesture, eye-pointing, expression, intonation and eventually spoken language. And they are using imitation all the time as they interact with others. In this social world children are surrounded by people who use talk in many, many different situations primarily in order to communicate. The talk children encounter in their homes and communities is talk for real purposes and between people who want to share meaning. There are no tests to fail or trick questions to answer. So the human infant, working hard to make and share meaning, does so in the supportive company of people who want to communicate with her. And you can be certain that this is true for all languages.

One of the most influential writers in the field of language acquisition was the American thinker and writer Noam Chomsky. He was the first to suggest that language acquisition is genetically determined. What he believed was that the human infant is born pre-programmed to work out the rules of speech or spoken language. If you think about it you will realise that speech – in any language – must be rule-governed if people are to be able to understand it, use it and be understood. There are rules in all languages. In English, for example, there are rules about the order of words. We can say 'the dog jumped over the fence' but if we say 'the fence jumped over the dog' it makes no sense because a fence cannot jump. If we say 'the jumped fence the over dog' we are uttering a string of exactly the same words but in an order that prevents it from being meaningful. The same rule does not necessarily apply to other languages. We also have rules about how we use verbs when we talk about the past tense. We say 'we walked' and 'we talked': the rule being that we add '-ed' to the end of the verb. And we have rules about how to talk about more than one object. We talk about shoes and socks and pens and pencils. The rule here is that we add the letter 's' to the end of a noun to make that noun plural. Importantly, however, there are exceptions to the rules. As a fluent speaker of the language you will know this. We say 'went' instead of 'goed' and 'flew' instead of 'flied': we talk of sheep instead of sheeps. Chomsky noticed that young children, having started out by saying things correctly through *imitating* what they have heard adults and fluent speakers say, then move on to making mistakes by applying the rules to all situations. Through listening they have worked out a rule that they then apply to all situations. Chomsky said the children were *over-generalising* the rules. In other words they worked out a rule at first through imitation and then applied it to everything – no exceptions. For Chomsky this was evidence that children are brilliant thinkers, working out the patterns they hear to make up the rules and then, logically, applying those rules to all situations.

It was these errors that suggested to Chomsky that children must have something that allows them to use the patterns they hear to work out the rules. What he proposed was that the *structure of language*, by which he meant the rules that bind it together to make it meaningful, depend on what he called a Language Acquisition Device (LAD). Language has to be rule-bound with the rules known to all for it to be used for sharing meaning. The rules that bind language together are its grammar. The LAD has, as its foundation, what Chomsky called a *universal grammar* or a linguistic *deep structure*, which he believed all humans are born with. The LAD is programmed to recognise, in the surface structure (i.e. the words and other features) of any statement or utterance, just how the deep structure will operate. So the surface features that are particular to that language (to English or Mandarin or isiZulu, for example) allow it to be operated by the universal blueprint. This is what accounts for the fact that *any human being is born capable of learning to communicate in any language. And in more than one language.* For Chomsky children are potentially competent users of language from birth and by competence he meant the underlying and unconscious knowledge of the rule system for generating language per se that human infants are born with. The errors, or the mistakes, children make show us the efforts they are making to find the patterns in the particular language, to work out the rules and apply them. Here are some examples to make this more clear:

> Fourteen-month-old Julia points to the animals in the field and says 'sheep'. Through imitating what she has heard others say she uses the correct plural. She has not yet worked out the pattern that operates in English for making plurals. One might be tempted to say that she is 'just copying'. But by the time she is 3 years old she labels the animals as 'sheeps'. She has moved on from making a grammatically correct response to making an error or mistake precisely because she has been paying attention to and analysing what she hears.

In essence this young child has worked out that adults have a pattern for making plurals: they add an 's' at the end of the word. Julia uses this pattern or rule to form all plurals as she hasn't yet learned what we know – that there are often exceptions to the rules. Language cannot be merely a repertoire or a range of responses since everything anyone utters or understands is a novel or new combination of words. When a child says something like 'The birds flied off' or 'I seed it and I feeled it and it's not a dog', each of these is a unique set of words, making meaning, but never before uttered by any human being. So the brain must hold a recipe or a programme or a blueprint that can build an infinite number of sentences out of a finite list of words. These are known as *mental grammars*.

Jerome Bruner was influenced by the work of Chomsky and saw it as taking thinking about how children acquire language as a leap forward from previous theories. His deep interest was in language, narrative and talk. He did, however, spot a gap in Chomsky's theory, which was the lack of any reference to other people, which means a lack of reference to interaction, culture or context. For Bruner, a sociocultural theorist, the development of language requires at least two people involved in negotiation. The purpose of language is communication and it is through communication that meaning is made and shared and fine-tuned. So, building on Chomsky's LAD, Bruner proposed a more sociocultural model which he called the Language Acquisition Support System (LASS). He conceived of this as a kind of adult scaffolding system. What happens is that children learn their language through their interactions with others, who cue the children's responses and share meanings with them in particular contexts and within cultures.

Bruner worked in both the USA and the UK and was very interested in the linguistic games and routines that occur between caregivers, particularly mothers, and infants in the early years. He noted that interactions like these were evident in all cultures and believed that they lay the essential foundations for the development of communicative systems. Bruner identified several ways in which the LASS helps the child move from prelinguistic (before spoken language) to linguistic communication. His focus was on what he called *formats*.

The first formats are the routine and familiar ones where the adult highlights the features of the world that are meaningful to the child. These formats have a basic or simple grammatical form. The features refer to the context or the situation. The interactions are often, but not necessarily, between mother and child and the formats are built around simple games. One of the formats Bruner analysed was the simple 'peekaboo' type of game with which you may be familiar. It is a common interactive game in the developed world but versions of it seem to appear throughout the world. In the game something or someone is present, then made to disappear and then reappear. This is usually accompanied by a verbal noise like 'boo!' (or its equivalent). The game has been made up by people and it follows a set pattern so that it is tied together by simple rules that can only vary slightly. The thing that disappears and reappears can change, as can whatever is used to make the disappearance happen, for example.

Bruner argued that games like these offer both the first occasions for the child to use language systematically with the adult and the first opportunity for the child to get something done with words. He described the games as being idealised and self-contained formats. In essence you can think about these game formats as having a deep structure and a set of rules and it is these rules that allow the surface of the game to be managed.

Let's analyse a peekaboo game where something is hidden and then reappears.

- The deep structure is the controlled disappearance and reappearance of the object or the person.
- The surface structure refers to all or any of the following: the screens or cloths or whatever is used to make the thing or person disappear and reappear; the timing of each act; the actual words or sounds used and the choice of what it is that is to disappear.
- The game is described as being 'nonnatural' – in the sense that it is invented or made up and it is tied together by the rules that can be negotiated.
- For us, in this book, concerned with language, we can think of these games as being like language in that they involve turn-taking roles that are not fixed but can be changed. It does not matter who hides: there is always a hider and a hidden, an actor and an experiencer. Bruner called these games

little *protoconversations*, which we can define as an interaction between an adult (typically a mother) and a baby that includes words, sounds and gestures, and attempts to convey *meaning* before the onset of spoken language in the child.

• The games provide opportunities for spreading attention over an ordered sequence of events. So the game itself is the topic or the theme about which each of the moves can be seen as a comment.

• Games like this do not occur in the animal world: they occur only in the human world and I would suggest that is because they are dependent on some use and exchange of language.

This has been what might be called a classic summary of thinking about language acquisition. Do remember that both Chomsky and Bruner were considering language acquisition by looking at children in the developed world.

It is important to add that much has been learned in recent years through the work on shared attention by such people as Colwyn Trevarthen and you might find this very revealing. His recent research (e.g. Malloch & Trevarthen, 2009) suggests that babies are innately musical, and have an excellent sense of rhythm, and even when a mother is not actually singing to a baby she tends to speak in a way that can be called musical so that the sounds of her words go up and down and with clear patterns of rhythm. What he notes is how precisely the baby responds – in coos and gestures – often exactly in time with the pulse and bar structure of her sounds. It is clear that infants learn by imitation but Trevarthen tells us that the structural foundations for imitative movements must be innate; when they imitate, some infants display remarkable precision from birth but there are large individual differences; at around 6 months of age an infant can be observed imitating signal gestures and mannerisms that have the characteristics of *protosigns* in protoconversations, with a shared grammar of action. The work 'proto' comes from the Greek and means first, earliest, original or naive.

Stephen Krashen (1988) believed that there is no fundamental difference between the way we acquire our first language and any subsequent languages. He, like Chomsky, thought that humans have an innate ability to process and learn language. The human infant learns her mother tongue simply by listening attentively to spoken language that is made meaningful to her through context. Other languages are acquired in the same way. When he started to consider the learning of a second or subsequent language Krashen drew up what he called the *Monitor Model*, which consists of a number of hypotheses:

• The *Acquisition-Learning Hypothesis*, which states that language can be either acquired or learned, and Krashen saw those as two different facilities. For him, acquisition was a sub-conscious process, like that of a child learning its own language or an adult 'picking up' a second language simply by living and working in another country. Learning, by contrast, he said was the conscious process of learning step by step through language lessons and a focus on grammar or rules.

- The *Natural Order Hypothesis* says that language is acquired in a predictable order by all learners. The order does not depend on the apparent simplicity or complexity of the grammatical features involved. This means that the natural order of acquisition will not be influenced by direct teaching of features that the learner is not yet ready to acquire.

- The *Monitor Hypothesis* says that we can use what we have already learned about the rules of a language by self-correcting the errors we think we have made. This may be more apparent in written language than in conversation.

- The *Input Hypothesis* says that it is possible for us to *acquire* language in one way only, which is when we are exposed to input (either written or spoken language) that is comprehensible to us. So comprehensible input is the necessary but also sufficient condition for language acquisition to take place. It requires no effort on the part of the learner. This is in line with the thinking about how young children learn best when what they are learning makes human sense to them.

- The *Affective Filter Hypothesis* states that language will not be acquired if the learner is suffering from anxiety, lack of motivation or low self-esteem.

Some people find these hypotheses and the distinction between acquisition and learning language contentious, but to give Krashen credit he was and remains a passionate advocate for retaining bilingualism during the years when, as we have seen, there was a strong move to insist that all children should use and learn only the official language. It was Krashen who noticed that many young bilinguals go through a *silent period* when they stay on the fringes of activities. This silence is not passivity. They are actively listening, thinking, almost drinking in the new language. So for me he is still a thinker to be reckoned with.

> Sofia, not yet 2 years old, lives part of the year in a village in Italy and part in Hong Kong. Her mother speaks Italian, her father is bilingual English/Italian and they are planning for her to learn some Mandarin when she starts nursery. When I saw her recently she was bright and communicative, understood everything said to her in both English and Italian, but did not utter a word of either language.
> (My observation notes on Dario Iacopucci's daughter, 2015)

> Six-year-old Abdul arrived in Stoke Newington on a Sunday night, having left his village home in Bangladesh the day before. His father brought him to school on Monday morning and left him there. Abdul spent weeks watching carefully, listening

attentively, copying what he saw others doing and sorting out the books in the book corner. Each day he would sort them by size or type or colour or whatever criterion he chose. And he said not one word. Until one day, about three months later when he came up to me, held up a picture he had drawn of his little sister and said 'Shahanara crying'. His silent period was over.

(Personal observation notes, 1980)

Many children acquire a second or a third language as a result of what happens in their lives. The languages they learn in addition to the one learned first (their mother tongue) may be essential to their ability to function in their daily lives. Selina Mushi tells us that a language may be considered a second language because '*its use in the surrounding environment is necessary for effective functioning in society (not necessarily because it is learned second in the sequence of learning languages)*' (2002a: 350).

Mellie Preston, a speaker of English, Spanish, Catalan and Italian, writes in her language history about how and why her children came to acquire their second and subsequent languages.

> My children, while my parents were alive they spoke and understood both Spanish and Catalan: we went back to Spain every two to three years while they were little and they had no problem communicating with their cousins and my cousins (I have 35 of them) and the rest of the family and friends.
>
> As I married an Australian man and he did not speak or understand anything other than English, it was quite hard to enforce the language with the kids as they grew older and we also felt that their Spanish heritage might have a negative connotation – they did not want to be labeled as 'wogs' so they refused to learn Spanish. My parents and the rest of the family in Spain would chastise me continuously for not teaching them Spanish. I wish I had listened to them!

We get a sense of just how complicated this world of more than one culture and language can be. How easy is it to decide which language is first, which second or whether a language was learned or acquired (in Krashen's terms)? Were the languages learned simultaneously or subsequently?

What we learn from this

We learn how brilliant the human infant is. All children acquire or learn their first languages without having to be taught them. They do this through their interactions with caregivers and others, by living with other people who are speakers of their languages, by imitating what they see and hear and by noticing patterns and identifying rules.

Section II

From the home and local community to the classroom or setting

'No child should be expected to cast off the language and culture of the home as he crosses the school threshold'

(The Bullock Report, 1975: 2)

In this section we move on from thinking about the personal to thinking about what happens beyond the home as the young child moves into a nursery setting or classroom. We look at:

- the place of language and languages in the early years curriculum;
- the pedagogical and social reasons for children being able to use their mother tongue or first language in their early learning;
- a brief history of minority education in Britain.

Chapter 5

Language/languages in the school curriculum

We learn almost everything we know through the language or languages we understand, speak, read, listen to, write, draw, paint, sing, narrate, question, understand, appreciate, explain and use. Loris Malaguzzi, founder of the famous early years provision in Reggio Emilia, called all the ways we have of expressing our feelings and ideas the *hundred languages*. Young children use these languages all the time as they make sense of their worlds and the people in them. In addition to reading and writing, spoken language has an ever-present and highly significant role in schools and settings. And for younger children, not yet reading and writing, talking and listening are vital. A good learning environment is one where there is a buzz of noise as learners share and compare ideas and experiences. A quiet early years room makes me uncomfortable – unless it is the time of the day when small children sleep.

In the UK the curriculum followed for young children is divided into two different sets of guidance: the *Early Years Foundation Stage* for children aged 2 to 5 and the *National Curriculum* for those aged 5 to 7. The place of language and languages in both is central in the sense that recognition is given to the importance of language to learning. All children are expected to be able to communicate verbally with adults and peers and learn to read and write. In the National Curriculum scant, if any, attention is paid to the particular learning needs of bilingual children. Educators are advised to take account of the needs of speakers of languages other than English but it is fluency in the English language that is demanded as an essential foundation for academic success in all subjects.

With younger children in mind, the *Early Years Foundation Stage* (September 2014) takes a more informed and culturally sensitive approach, stating that:

> 1.7. For children whose home language is not English, providers must take reasonable steps to provide opportunities for children to develop and use their home language in play and learning, supporting their language development at home.

Providers must also ensure that children have sufficient opportunities to learn and reach a good standard in English language during the EYFS: ensuring children are ready to benefit from the opportunities available to them when they begin Year 1. When assessing communication, language and literacy skills, practitioners must assess children's skills in English. If a child does not have a strong grasp of English language, practitioners must explore the child's skills in the home language with parents and/or carers, to establish whether there is cause for concern about language delay.

(DfE, 2014: 9)

This is a small but important concession to the learning needs of the numbers of children in early years settings who have languages other than English and accepting the need for encouraging and allowing them to use these languages in both the home and the school or setting.

In the United States, Nancy Hornberger and Holly Link (2012) critically reviewed *No Child Left Behind* (2001), Obama's reauthorisation of the *Elementary and Secondary Education Act*, and designed to be the government's flagship aid programme for disadvantaged students. Well-intentioned but, in reality, standardised tests still dominate what is taught and how it is taught; first language literacy is discouraged and bilingual students who engage in code-switching or translanguaging are undervalued. Hornberger and Link (2012) cite a case study in which we are told that the school in question offers rich and varied language practices such as the use of what they call 'transnational' literacies and translanguaging. These are welcomed and celebrated as part of the curriculum in order to enable the bilingual students to succeed in formal education. Hornberger and her colleagues are more usually involved in examining secondary schooling so we look at only one case study − that of first-grade Beatriz.

She had moved from Guerrero in Mexico to a peri-urban town (meaning a town which retains links with the surrounding countryside) outside of Philadelphia with her mother and two older siblings to join her father, who had arrived there several years earlier. She had been only 3 years old at the time of the move. The town the family moved to was one with an increasing number of Latinos, most of whom were recent immigrants to the area. The school she went to was one with very little experience of bilingualism or of exposure to Latino children until recent years when more and more Spanish-speaking, Mexican-origin or Mexican-heritage children arrived. The language of instruction at the school was English but the classrooms were fast becoming multilingual spaces as children from both Spanish and non-Spanish speaking households met to speak to one another and learn bits of Spanish for a variety of functions throughout the school day.

Hornberger and Link describe Beatriz's experience during the equivalent of our literacy hour like this:

> Beatriz sits on the rug with her first grade classmates, listens to a story read in English, and then discusses it in both Spanish and English with a peer. When called on, she offers, in English, a complete sentence about the story's setting. Shortly after, she and several students leave to attend their daily English as a Second Language (ESL) class upstairs in the library during which time she participates in guided, leveled reading in English, and chats with her friends in Spanish and English while completing spelling work in English.
>
> (2012: 269)

Later and back in her classroom she joins a group at the computers to practise rhyming words in English, then reads and talks about an English book with two friends, one a bilingual Spanish/English speaker and the other an English speaker. They talk about the story and then together devise and write some sentences in English, and Beatriz and her Spanish friend teach some of the other children a few Spanish words. At lunchtime she goes with a newly arrived Mexican student to the lunchroom and interprets from English to Spanish for her as they walk through the cafeteria line. At break time she and a small group of girls sing and play hand games – some English and some Spanish – which she carries on playing on the school bus trip home. Back home she greets her baby sister, tells her mum about her day in Spanish and translates some documents for her about upcoming school events. She then goes outside with her siblings to meet up with neighbourhood friends and they sit out there drawing and writing; chatting and calling out to passersby in English and Spanish. Later the school-age children sit at the dining room table and complete their homework, writing in English and discussing spelling and maths in both languages.

There is more to her day, which you can read about in the article.

What we get from this is a picture of this child's *communicative repertoires*, the way she uses her languages for different functions, with different people and for different purposes. She is like most of the young bilingual children we encounter in our schools and settings. The point of citing this example is to identify what it is that has enabled this child to cope with English as the sole language of instruction. Hornberger and Link (2012) tell us that it is the teachers' positive attitude towards the use of Spanish (and by implication any other language) in the classroom that allows all this to happen. Spanish is not only allowed but celebrated. This overt respect for children's linguistic skills legitimises their use of what they bring from home, things both academic and social. It is significant that to all intents and purposes this is becoming a bilingual community – Spanish and English. In this school there are only two languages to consider and that makes it very different from schools which need to deal with speakers of many different languages.

Let us look at another and very different case study, this time from a kindergarten named WNT and located in a poor community in Napier in New Zealand. The researchers were Haworth *et al.* (2006).

In June 2003, Wycliffe Nga Tamariki (WNT) Kindergarten in Napier was selected as one of six national Centres of Innovation to become involved in a 3-year programme of action research funded by the New Zealand Ministry of Education. The idea of a national government body sponsoring a long term action research programme in early childhood seems remote from what happens here. These six centres all stated that their aims were to '*identify, enhance and disseminate innovative teaching and learning practices, in line with the national strategic plan in early childhood education*' (Ministry of Education, 2002: 297). A special feature of the WNT context was the successful and long-term partnership that had been established with the local Samoan community and, as a result, a group of Samoan children regularly joined the afternoon sessions in WNT. To start with, only a few young Samoan children attended but later a new building was constructed and became a licensed early childhood centre in 2004. Most of the children at WNT came from English-speaking backgrounds. English is also the language spoken in the homes of the Maori or the indigenous culture.

> The children from Upu Amata, whose home language is Samoan, make up the smallest group in the afternoon sessions; however, their presence has impacted strongly on the ethos of the WNT context. This factor had a strong influence on the kindergarten's selection as a Centre of Innovation. Hence, a special focus in this project has been to identify those factors influencing Samoan children's bilingual development and to explore ways to further enhance this within the WNT setting.
> (Ministry of Education, 2002: 298)

All three teachers and full-time teaching assistants are palagi (which means non- Samoan). English is therefore the dominant language of communication used by teachers. But three languages – English, Samoan and the indigenous Maori language – are regularly included in the WNT programme. A bilingual Samoan teaching assistant also comes to the afternoon sessions, to offer invaluable support for teachers as well as enriching the linguistic environment for all children. The kindergarten's programme is guided by New Zealand's famous early childhood curriculum, *Te Whāriki* (Ministry of Education, 1996), which is underpinned by a strong sociocultural philosophy that supports an integrated, holistic approach to learning. This is not a place of a skills or a subject-based curriculum, but a true early childhood programme. A place where children are invited to ask questions and find answers, build on their prior experience, languages and cultures, and that values all contributions children bring. It also emphasises the '*critical role of socially and culturally mediated learning and of reciprocal and responsive relationships for children with people, places and things*' (Ministry of Education, 1996: 9). The adults consciously interact with all the children in ways that support and promote their learning, particularly that of young bilingual children.

Haworth *et al.* (2006) tell us what insights the research gave them into the learning and development of young bilingual learners. These are summarised here. You can read them in full in the article itself.

The first is the *importance of mediation* in the process of allowing children to learn a second language whilst retaining the first. Mediation, you will know, is similar to scaffolding.

> A mediator facilitates the child's development by making it easier for the child to perform a certain behaviour. In the Vygotskian framework, mediators become mental tools.... Like other cultural tools, mediators exist first in shared activity and then are appropriated by the child.... Overt mediators function as scaffolding, helping the child make the transition from maximum assisted performance to independent performance.
>
> (Bodrova & Leong, 1996: 69–70)

The mediators who were seen as being essential to the bilingual development of the children include adults, peers, cultural tools, language and the children themselves. Here is the headteacher Heather, giving an example of *adult mediation*:

> Peteru and Heather were working on the computer when all of a sudden Peteru has another idea. He starts pointing to parts of Heather's face and asking 'what is that?' Heather answers his questions by naming eyes, ears, nose, and mouth in English. Now Heather points to the same parts of Peteru's face. He replies mata, taliga, isu, gutu. As the conversation continues, Peteru does not know the Samoan word for jacket, so Heather and Peteru ask a Samoan adult in the Kindergarten. They are told it could be ofu faatimu. Both Peteru and Heather repeat this new word several times.
>
> (Haworth et al., 2006: 301)

Here an older Samoan *child mediates* by giving the appropriate words to her younger peers during a cooking session. Linda, a teaching assistant, is present.

> Linda: That's right, pour it into the measuring cup. [Pele goes to pour it into the measuring cup].
> Linda: Oh, great pouring!
> [Mareta comes over to where Pele is working and has a look].
> Mareta: O fea ni vai? (Where's the water?)

Salesi: Sole ki ifo gi ou? Sole Mareta ki ifo gio'u vai?
(Hey, can you pour? Hey, Mareta, can you pour some water in mine?)
Linda: Oh, Mareta, you are a helper! [as Mareta obliges].

(Haworth *et al.*, 2006: 301)

Cultural tools can mediate in young children's developing bilingualism. They are the things produced within a culture to share meanings and include books, paintings, artefacts, pens and pencils and much more. They may equate with Malaguzzi's hundred languages. Here, one of the teachers, Pam, explains how music and song or *cultural tools can mediate* in children's developing bilingualism at WNT.

> Each day at approximately 2pm we have a group gathering or mat-time for all the children that attend our afternoon session. We play music (usually Samoan) to call the children to the mat. Then we play music from any of the three cultures at WNT (Maori, English or Samoan) for movement games.
>
> After greeting the people working in the kindergarten in Samoan (talofa) or in Maori language (kia ora) we sing Tena Koe (a greeting, in Maori, to one person). We follow this with a Samoan Greeting song. The children are encouraged to stand up and move around the circle shaking one another's hand, whilst still singing.
>
> After a story it is time for fruit (we often refer to this, in Maori, as kai time). Before we eat, we sing the Grace in both Maori and Samoan.

(Haworth *et al.*, 2006: 302–303)

Language itself can mediate in young children's developing bilingualism. The researchers believe that language input is, in itself, a mediator in young children's developing bilingualism. We know that language is a cultural tool and it is used in songs and poetry, stories and rhymes, all of which are embedded in a culture. Listening to these and joining in with them allows children to identify patterns and ideas and work out rules and conventions about languages and how they work. In the research they looked at private speech and translanguaging.

What we learn from this

We learn that it is important that we know what languages the children speak (and possibly read and write) and that we make them know that we recognise and value their linguistic skills. We learn too that when we invite children to use their languages in whatever way they can we boost their self-esteem and make it more likely that they will become valued and full participants of the culture we are building in our classes and settings.

And we learn that adults, other children, language itself and cultural tools can mediate the learning and development of young bilingual children.

Chapter 6

Why young children should use their first language throughout their early years

This chapter is an important one because it is addressing perhaps the key issue in the education of young bilingual learners. I have based much of this on the report for UNESCO called *Enhancing Learning of Children from Diverse Language Backgrounds: Mother tongue-based bilingual or multilingual education in the Early Years*, written by Jessica Ball (2011) from the University of Victoria.

The review starts with an overview of theory and research, some of which has already been touched on in this book. In the literature on this subject there seems to be an agreement amongst theorists and researchers that young children's abilities to learn languages and become literate are affected by their sociocultural environments (where they live, what their parents do and so on) as well as by the languages they are exposed to and how they have been socialised into these by their parents and carers. We know that almost all young children learn their first languages in the naturalistic settings and emotional warmth of their homes. They learn from listening and attending to the events – the routines and rituals – that make up everyday lives. In these situations everything is meaningful to the child because the purpose is clear. The child is treated as an equal participant, listened to and paid attention to. This style of *intimate interaction* is very different from what the child encounters in a school or setting. And there are things from the child's culture that affect her and her language in myriad ways. These include the songs that are sung to her, the books looked at, the stories listened to, the games played. This is true for all children, but for children whose culture is not the one of school or setting it is unlikely that she will have much to draw on which will be recognised or appreciated by the practitioners.

Most of the children who arrive at school with some competence in more than one language will probably have grown up bilingual or multilingual from their earliest days at home. They have not experienced *successive acquisition* – which means formally learning a second or third language. There are studies showing that children can learn three or more languages starting in their early years and some theorists suggest that, with sufficient motivation, exposure, periods of formal study and opportunities for practice, children can ultimately become proficient in several languages. We have seen this in our language histories. Becoming bilingual is not easy and there are myths about young children being able to '*soak up languages like a sponge*'. In reality language acquisition takes a long time (Collier, 1989; Cummins, 1991) and may not always be successful. There are many factors involved in this.

There is another myth which says that young children can acquire a second or additional language faster than older children but, as Lightbown (2008) says, becoming completely fluent in a second language is not simple but necessarily takes several years. The message for us in this is that it would be wrong to think that offering children the opportunity to learn a second language in the early years will prepare them for academic success in that language. There is evidence that some educators, parents and policy makers believe that a child's first language will suffer when the child begins to learn a second language (as suggested in Smith, 1931). This is only likely to happen if the support for her continuing to use her mother tongue is withdrawn. Young children need to continue to use their mother tongue whilst they are learning a second language. We need to remember the growing evidence which shows that early bilingualism can provide children with benefits that go beyond knowing more than one language.

Here is a summary of what we learn from the literacy.

1   From research we learn that *bilingual children typically develop certain types of cognitive flexibility and metalinguistic awareness earlier and better than their monolingual peers* (e.g. Bialystok, 2001; Cummins, 2000; King & Mackey, 2007).

2   *Young children will learn a second language in different ways depending upon their culture and the status of their culture, language and community within their larger social setting.* So we need to be able to distinguish which children are members of a minority ethnolinguistic group (sometimes called minority language children) and which are members of a majority ethnolinguistic group (majority language children); and among those within each group who are learning bilingually from infancy versus those who have learned a single mother tongue and are learning a second or additional language later in childhood. We also might need to think about indigenous children who, in many cases, will not be learning the mother tongue of their ancestors as their first language because they will be learning the language of the dominant culture. Their heritage languages may have already died out or fallen into the group of languages threatened with extinction (Ball, 2011).

3   *Parents and other primary caregivers have the strongest influence on children's first language acquisition in the early years.* They are the child's first teachers and there are dangers of making judgements about their skills as teachers because of having some definition of what could be defined as a universal 'good

parent' in mind. All we know is that all parents do the best that they can. Parents very often need additional information to enable them to make informed decisions. From the language histories you will have encountered parents who wanted children to retain their first language in order to keep their culture and their links to family, ancestors, the past and traditions. We also encountered those who felt it was essential to learn the dominant language at any price in order to succeed academically, economically and socially in this new society. Lao's (2004) study of English-Chinese bilingual preschoolers underscores the important contributions of parents' home language behaviour in supporting preschool children's first language development. She says that mother tongue development cannot be achieved without a strong commitment from parents. To enable parents to facilitate their children's home language and literacy skills, she urges the provision of meaningful print-rich home environments, guidance from adults with high levels of literacy, partnerships with schools, and support for parents who need to improve their own oral and written skills in L1. We might be tempted to describe her as a 'tiger mum' but her advice is sound.

The UNESCO report (Ball, 2011) sees the issue of the role of parents in bilingual education as crucial and summarises their recommendations like this:

- Parents and carers may need to be helped, through different programmes of support, to see the value for children to continue using their mother tongues in the years of early education. They may need to be reassured that, despite the possibility of some initial delay in learning and using a second language, the child is more likely to succeed academically when mother tongue use is encouraged. And parents should be encouraged to continue using L1 in the home.
- Those training to teach should be reminded that children's individual differences in learning styles, capacities, interests, motivation and temperament may significantly affect the speed and quality of their language acquisition.

4   *Young children's abilities to learn languages and subsequently develop early reading and writing skills are affected by their home circumstances or their sociocultural environments.* Their language development will thus be determined by the language or languages spoken by their parents and family members and by the ways in which languages are used within their culture. Young children will be influenced by what they hear in terms of the styles and registers used by their parents and carers. In her important book on language and class, called *Ways with Words*, Shirley Brice Heath (1983) studied the language usage in two contrasting groups in the USA and examined the effect of the language used within the homes on the requirements of formal education. She was not considering bilingualism but language per se.

Teachers often interpreted silence from immigrant children as ignorance or resistance. Homework, especially assignments involving extended multimodal projects, embarrassed immigrant parents whose inability to help their children meant that they lost respect in their children's eyes. These parents saw their dreams for what American education could provide their children begin to slip away as they stood by, watching helplessly as their children gravitated more and more to peer interactions away from home.

(Heath, 1983: 18–19)

This is such a common theme of many books and stories and songs – and you find echoes of it in the language histories of people like Hong-Bich. Some of the children of immigrants, despite speaking the same language as that of the school, may still be alienated because the type of spoken language of the home differs from that of the school. Mushi (2002a) tells us that *early bilingualism can provide children with benefits that go beyond knowing more than one language.*

5   *There is much evidence that bilingual children develop particular skills with regard to using language, including cognitive flexibility and metalinguistic awareness, earlier and more successfully than their monolingual peers.* Diaz (1983) cites studies which suggest that the cognitive flexibility noted in bilinguals could be seen where young children do such things as use spoken language when engaged in non-verbal tasks or use language in ways more sophisticated than those used by monolingual children.

6   *In addition to the cognitive advantages of becoming bilingual, there are the emotional and social advantages of being able to continue to be a fully participant member of your family, past and present, and your culture.*

One of the most powerful writers on the subject of multilingualism was and still is Tove Skutnabb-Kangas who, together with Jim Cummins, wrote a wonderful book called *Minority Education: From Shame to Struggle* (1988) in which she argued personally and passionately for the retention of the mother tongue. Her arguments relate very closely to the significance of language to identity, sense of belonging, and community. Here is some of what she said:

Many minority children are being forced to feel ashamed of their mother tongue, their parents, their origins, their group and their culture. Many of them, especially in countries where the racism is more subtle, not so openly expressed, take over the negative views which the majority society has of the minority groups, their languages and cultures. Many disown their parents and their own group and language. They shift identity 'voluntarily' and want to be German, Dutch, American, British, Swedish, etc.

(Skutnabb-Kangas & Cummins, 1988: 18)

She was writing a long time ago and mainly about older children but the warning is clear and worth considering.

7   *Bilingualism has positive effects on children's linguistic and educational development. We need not only to know this but to be able to explain it to the parents, colleagues, the children themselves.* Cummins (2001) says that when children and their languages are welcomed by educators and they are enabled to develop their abilities in two or more languages throughout their early years in school or setting, they gain a deeper understanding of language as a tool – an essential cognitive tool – and how to use it effectively. Where they are learning also to read and write they are gaining more practice in processing language. What this means is that they are able to compare and contrast the ways in which their two languages organise reality.

8   *The level of competence in the first language is a strong predictor of how the second language will develop.* The clear implication of this is that where a child comes to school speaking fluently and confidently in her mother tongue she will develop both her linguistic and early literacy skills in the school language. Those children who have been told and read stories, heard songs and had conversations with family members in their mother tongue are being given the foundation for learning the language of school or setting. It is important to remember that this applies to all languages. There is no language that does not enable children to be able to communicate, understand, explain, question and make sense of the world.

We now examine some examples and case studies of schools and settings offering programmes specifically designed (or not) to meet the needs of bilingual children. Bilingual and multilingual programmes in schools are being implemented in countries around the globe and Somalia, Madagascar, Guinea Conakry, Burkina Faso, Cameroon, Tanzania, China, Ethiopia, Guatemala, the Philippines and South Africa are just a few of these. A variety of models of bilingual or multilingual teaching take place in this.

The table on page 54 is adapted from the one in the UNESCO report (Ball, 2011), which shows you different approaches to bilingual education.

Mother-tongue based instruction	The teaching programme is delivered entirely in L1
Bilingual or two-way bilingual education	Here two languages may be used by the teachers and practitioners and children. This dual language teaching means all children are taught in both languages
Mother-tongue based bilingual education or developmental education	Here mother tongue or L1 is the primary medium for teaching for the whole of the school/setting and L2 is introduced as a subject to prepare the children for transition at a later stage to some academic subjects in L2
Multilingual education	In this model there is the formal use of more than two languages in the curriculum. This is taking place in parts of South Africa
Transitional bi/ multilingual education also called bridging	The aim is to have a planned transition from one language of instruction to another Short cut or early exit are terms for programmes that involve an abrupt transition to L2 instruction after only 2 or 3 years in school Late transition or late exit refers to a switch to L2 instruction after a child has become fully fluent academically in L1
Maintenance bi/multilingual education	After L2 has been introduced both or all languages are media of instruction. L1 instruction continues, often as a subject of study, to ensure ongoing support for children to become academically proficient in L1. This is also called additive bilingual education because one or more languages are added but do not replace L1
Immersion or foreign language instruction	The whole programme is provided in a language that is new to the child
Submersion or sink or swim	This is the most anti-child but still common in some places. Speakers of the non-dominant languages have no choice other than having to learn through a language they do not understand. It promotes subtractive bilingualism, which means the child learns a second language at the expense of the first

Source: Adapted from Ball (2011).

It is estimated that, in developing countries, 221 million children enter the classroom or setting unable to understand or speak the language they are and will be taught in. All of these millions of children will be experiencing models like those outlined in the table above. Many countries that were colonised still teach in the old colonial language, while in other countries the language of schools and settings may well be the dominant national or international language, neither of which many young children will speak at home. This means that children are put in the impossible position of trying to decipher what they are being taught in an unknown language.

The children facing the greatest difficulty are those living in remote rural areas and speaking a language at home that is not the one of the school or setting. It may be a language absolutely new to them, one they have never before heard. It is, of course, important for children to become fluent in the new language, but the question is whether this should be at the expense of the mother tongue.

9 *Cummins (2001) tells us that the bilingual child's two languages are interdependent.* This means that the transfer across languages can be two-way: when the mother tongue is promoted in the school or setting – as in places operating a bilingual education programme the concepts, language and literacy skills that the child is learning in the majority or school language can transfer to the home language. It is as though one language feeds the other, but this is only the case where home and setting give children permission, support and access to using both languages.

10 *Encouraging and supporting the use of mother tongue in the school or setting helps develop not only the mother tongue but also the child's abilities in the majority school language.* You will not find this surprising in view of the previous findings that (a) bilingualism confers linguistic advantages on children and (b) abilities in the two languages are significantly related or interdependent. Bilingual children perform better in school when the school effectively teaches the mother tongue and, where appropriate, develops literacy in that language. By contrast, when children are encouraged to reject their mother tongue and not use it, its development stagnates and they lose confidence in themselves and in learning. Where teaching the mother tongue is not feasible there must be every attempt to respect and encourage the use of mother tongue in the setting (based on Cummins, 2001:17).

It is important to think about just how fragile children's mother tongues are and how easily lost. You have only to think about children being teased or bullied or excluded or made to feel stupid because their language is not that of the majority. You will find examples of language loss in many of the language histories.

A reminder: rejecting a child's language is tantamount to rejecting the child. You are suggesting that the child and her language and her family and her culture are not welcome in your class and setting.

What we learn from this

We learn just how important it is that children are encouraged and supported to use their first languages in the school or setting and how important it is that we are able to explain this to parents. We need to find ways of involving parents in understanding what we are doing and why. Only in this way can we rely on their support. We have learned too that the support of parents and carers is essential to children's successful learning.

Chapter 7

A brief history of minority education in the UK

To contextualise where we are now in terms of supporting the learning of young bilingual children in this country we need to consider how we got to be where we are today. We have, in our schools and settings throughout the country, many thousands of children who speak and sometimes read and write more than one language. They bring with them the richness of more than one culture. Contained in this richness are their individual language histories, including the songs and books and stories and rhymes and games and music and customs and rituals they have experienced. The children bring with them resources often unknown to us, which could offer us links to build on. In historic terms multiculturalism and multilingualism are relatively new realities and understanding how they came about and how successive governments viewed them is important to our understanding of what we did in this country to welcome and support these ethnic minority children in our schools and settings.

Mass immigration into the UK began after World War II, when poor and hungry peoples from devastated Europe and from the West Indies and South Asia arrived in the country, some as political refugees, others as economic migrants, seeking work in order to survive. It was the start of Britain, as the host country, having to address the issue that is so contentious today – that of immigration and its impact. The first immigrants began to arrive in large numbers in the late 1940s and legislation was first passed to stem this immigration in the 1960s. This legislation allowed for both entry and stay for some categories of workers and their dependents. Afro-Caribbean immigrants were the first to bring their wives and children with them and were gradually followed in doing this by immigrants from India, Pakistan and Bangladesh, the majority of whom achieved family reunification in the 1970s, 1980s and 1990s respectively. So ethnic minority children started to come into British schools and settings in significant numbers in the early 1950s.

How the children were regarded and educated in those early years was determined by decisions made on educational grounds but also on the political dogma, racist thinking and public opinion of the time. If you read novels or watch movies about this period it is evident that in those early days many regarded immigration as being problematic: it was seen as a threat to the established culture of white Britain. You may well have seen films or read about landlords in cities putting notices in the windows of houses saying things like 'No dogs. No children. No Blacks' or 'No Irish'. Anything like that would be illegal nowadays but under the surface veneer of tolerance you may find that not much has changed when one thinks of current rhetoric about immigration. The immigrants were seen as being alien, foreign and ignorant largely because they could not speak English. They were stereotyped and often rejected. A whole culture of overt racism and denigration began.

In the mid-1960s the effect of having children of other colours and religions, speaking languages other than English in British schools began to be discussed and it is important to remember that in the midst of all the negative voices there were some educationalists and others who did attempt to challenge racial stereotypes and build a positive multicultural and multilingual climate within which children could be helped to live and learn together. But looking back we can see how narrow some of the thinking behind the approaches adopted was. Take, for example, those who recommended seeing all children as being the same. This is an approach that some, during the era of black consciousness, called the '*colour-blind humanism of Martin Luther King*'. Some argued that the way to show respect for other cultures was to introduce things related to the cultures within classrooms by placing chopsticks and 'ethnic' dressing up clothes in the home corner, the odd book in another language in the library and celebrate Eid or Diwali. It took time and awareness before teachers, practitioners, parents and children themselves recognised that they were being patronised, othered, silenced and discriminated against and, although decades have passed and a range of positive moves made, it is clear that many children still face the negative and damaging effects of racism. If your language and culture are not recognised as having the same value as those of your peers, aspects of your very identity are being denigrated.

It is very important to think carefully about racism and I can think of no one who has thought and written more powerfully about racism than the late Stuart Hall. He reminds us that human beings have had a need to divide human society up into categories according to physical attributes and other defining features. It is one way in which we classify things in order to make sense of the world. Until you classify people according to some criteria the complexity of society seems too difficult to manage. So we sort people by gender, by race, by religion, by class, by ability, by social status and more. Hall tells us that this classifying is '*an absolutely fundamental aspect of human culture*' (1997: 2). To classify is fine, but what happens when the groups classified are then ranked and the issue of power comes into play? Most of us will have seen examples of this when we look at the history of women, of gay people, of people with learning difficulties. Hall goes on to say:

> you know, it's not just that you have blacks and whites, but of course one group of those people have a much more positive value than the other group. That's how power operates. But then, anything that attempts to ascribe to the black population, characteristics that used to be used for the white ones, generates enormous tension in the society.
>
> (1997: 3)

In a way this kind of classification keeps everything in its place. We all know who we are, according to how we have been classified. But what happens if a black person has attributes or aspirations to be more like white people? Mary Douglas, the anthropologist, calls this '*matter out of place*'. It is a little like expecting people to 'know their place' and stay there. When a group that has been discriminated against seeks to raise its status in society they are seen to be challenging the status quo.

Immigrant children, black and white, were all classified as being immigrants and hence different from 'us'. We almost anticipated and expected them to fail in our schools because they did not speak English nor share our culture. I can remember in the early 1970s when young Chinese children began to surprise teachers by doing so very well in school. They were challenging the status quo but also, in a small way, paving the way for others to join them.

It was only in the 1970s with the rise of black power groups that the negative impact of racism was openly acknowledged and attempts were made to address and redress it. West Indian parents had for long been angered that their children were routinely failing in the system, with a disproportionate number finding themselves in schools described as for the 'educationally subnormal'. Outraged about this they began to make demands for it to be dealt with. After decades, the Labour government of the time, in a report on *The West Indian Community* (SCRRI, 1977), highlighted these widespread concerns about the poor performance of West Indian children in schools and recommended that the government should institute a high level and independent inquiry into the causes of this underachievement. The then Labour eduction secretary, Shirley Williams, set up the *Committee of Inquiry into the Education of Children from Ethnic Minority Groups*, which was asked to do the following:

• *examine factors outside of the formal school system* which might affect the children's results, including influences in early childhood and prospects for school leavers;

- consider how to put in place *systems for monitoring and reviewing the progress of* these pupils and
- *recommend how best to fund all this.*

Anthony Rampton, the chair of the committee, was a philanthropist, humanitarian, gifted photographer and painter and his task was far from easy. He urged the committee to avoid superficial explanations and asked them to look at the contentious issues of low teacher expectations and racial prejudice among white teachers and society as a whole. One gets the sense that he was able to see that it was racism within the teaching body and the host society that led to low expectations of what the 'black' children could achieve. The committee, while willing to look at those issues, failed to consider and examine issues such as social class and the impact of poverty on the children's performance. As you can imagine, this message was no more popular then than it is in some circles even today. The media criticised the report and, with Thatcher then in office, Rampton was sacked and the final report was published in 1985. You can read more about the report at: www.educationengland.org.uk/documents/rampton/.

Rampton was then replaced by Michael Swann, a biologist who had played active senior roles at various universities in England and Scotland. Thirty members served on the committee and their report was submitted to Conservative education secretary Keith Joseph in March 1985. It was a substantial report, although complaints were and still are made about its many errors and inaccuracies.

Here is a summary of the some of the main recommendations. As you read it remember that a primary aim of the report was to change behaviour and attitudes:

- the focus should have been on how to educate not only ethnic minority children but all children;
- children, their parents, teachers, schools, settings and all educators need to recognise that Britain is and will remain a multiracial, multicultural and, by implication, multilingual country;
- education must not only reinforce the beliefs, values and identity that each child brings to school but must be alert and able to combat racism, and challenge and attack inherited myths and stereotypes;
- multicultural understanding must permeate all aspects of a school's work – it is not a separate topic that can be welded on to existing practices;
- there should be a system of a non-denominational and undogmatic approach to religious education;
- groups of children should not be taught exclusively by teachers of the same ethnic group;
- the under-representation of ethnic minorities in the teaching profession is a matter for great concern;

- the most important potential source of ethnic minority teachers in the future are the ethnic minority pupils currently in school. Careers teachers and careers officers, with the strong support of DES and HMI, should encourage ethnic minority youngsters to consider the possibility of entering teaching.

Some of the Swann Report (1985) or *Education for All* (as the report was called) looks good at first glance. But a critical reading reveals how it has subtly shifted the focus from racism to the more gentle 'inclusive multiculturalism'.

As someone interested and/or involved in early childhood education you need to be alert to searching beneath the surface so that you are able to really critically evaluate what you read. The Swann Report is full of fine sounding words but from what you have read of it and in light of your own experiences do you feel it adequately addresses the complex web of issues that continue to disadvantage certain groups of children? Is it wise to skirt around the very real impact of racism, prejudice, stereotyping, the impact of poverty and the advantages and disadvantages of bilingualism?

As a footnote to all this you might like to consider the impact of another aspect of the report – the rejection of the idea of separate 'ethnic minority schools', particularly Islamic schools. Remember that at that time there were Anglican, Catholic and Jewish schools and these were regarded as perfectly acceptable. What sort of message was given to the Islamic community? And what effect is that having today? It is clear that the Swann Report did prompt a high profile academic debate about the relative merits of multicultural and antiracist education. Yet as in many debates about vital issues nothing much has been resolved. There is not space in this book to go into the ongoing debate in any detail but I suggest that if this interests you, turn to Issa and Hatt's book *Language, Culture and Identity in the Early Years* (2013).

The Bullock Report or *A Language for Life* was set up by the Committee of Enquiry, appointed in 1972 by Margaret Thatcher, Secretary of State for Education in Ted Heath's Conservative government, and asked to consider, in relation to schools, the following:

- all aspects of teaching the use of English, including reading, writing and speech;
- how present practice might be improved and the role that initial and in-service teacher training might play;
- to what extent arrangements for monitoring the general level of attainment in these skills can be introduced or improved; and to make recommendations.

Here is a summary of the report's main recommendations. See if you can find in this summary anything relating to languages other than English. It recommended:

1 a system of monitoring should be introduced covering a wider range of attainments than has been attempted in the past and including new criteria for the definition of literacy;

2 steps should be taken to develop the language ability of children in the preschool and nursery and infant years;

3 every school should devise a systematic policy for the development of reading competence in pupils of all ages and ability levels;

4 each school should have an organised policy for language (but no mention of languages) across the curriculum;

5 every school should have a suitably qualified teacher with responsibility for advising and supporting colleagues in language and the teaching of reading;

6 there should be close consultation and communication between schools to ensure continuity in the teaching of reading and in the language development of every pupil;

7 English in the secondary school should have improved resources in terms of staffing, accommodation and ancillary help;

8 every Local Education Authority (LEA) should appoint a specialist English adviser and establish an advisory team with the specific responsibility of supporting schools in all aspects of language in education;

9 LEAs and schools should introduce early screening procedures to prevent cumulative language and reading failure and to guarantee individual diagnosis and treatment;

10 additional assistance should be given to children retarded in reading, and where pupils are withdrawn from classes for special help they should receive appropriate support on their return;

11 every LEA should have a reading clinic or remedial centre, offering a comprehensive diagnostic service and expert medical, psychological, teaching help and an advisory service to schools in association with the LEA's specialist adviser;

12 provision for the tuition of adult illiterates and semi-literates should be greatly increased, and there should be a national reference point for the co-ordination of information and support;

13 *children of families of overseas origin should have more substantial and sustained tuition in English. More advisers and specialist teachers are needed in areas of need*;

14 a standing working party with DES and LEA representatives should consider capitation allowances and the resources of schools – a satisfactory level of book provision should be its first subject of inquiry;

15 a substantial course on language in education (including reading) should be part of every primary and secondary school teacher's initial training;

16 there should be more in-service education opportunities in reading and other aspects of English teaching, including courses at diploma and higher degree level;

17   there should be a national centre for language in education, concerned with the teaching of English in all its aspects, from language and reading in the early years to advanced studies with sixth forms.

Did you notice what a deficit model seemed to be in the minds of the writers in their use of language – terms such as retarded, remedial, illiterate, semi-literate? Was this really such a different country then that only one out of 17 recommendations even mentions children 'of overseas origin'? And the words bilingual, monolingual, multilingual do not even appear. But read on. This, for me, was a painful lesson in how important it is to check the facts and read carefully. The Bullock Report has the subtitle of *A Language for Life* and it was this title, plus reading the book *Young Bilingual Children in Nursery School* (2000) written by Linda Thompson that persuaded me to read the whole report and not just the recommendations.

And look at what I discovered. Here are some extracts from the report and I think you will find them surprising. You may be tempted to skim read what follows but I urge you to read carefully because it is full of wise and still important and relevant ideas.

> 20.2 … In 1973 … there were 284,754 'immigrant children' in maintained primary and secondary schools in England and Wales, comprising 3.3% of the total school population. More significantly, since immigrant populations are concentrated largely upon Greater London and industrial cities in the Midlands and North, individual local education authorities can have as high a proportion of immigrant children on roll as 27%. Raw statistics such as these help to show why such a large measure of attention has to be paid in some areas, much more than in others, to the educational needs of the children labelled 'immigrant'. Obviously what is needed is as sharp a measure as possible of these special educational needs. **An immigrant child does not present problems to a school simply because he is an immigrant child.** Centrally collected figures cannot, for instance, indicate exactly the numbers of children with linguistic needs nor give any measure of these needs. The only people who can do this satisfactorily are the people on the spot, the teachers in the schools and the local education authorities. A few authorities have already had considerable practice in making such assessments. Bradford is notable in having carried out for several years an annual survey of immigrant children in its schools, distinguishing between their different ethnic origins, identifying their levels of proficiency in English, and making flexible educational arrangements accordingly. **We recommend that all authorities with immigrant children should make similar surveys regularly, in order to achieve a greater refinement in their educational arrangements.**

> 20.3 The term 'immigrant' is sometimes used in a very general sense, often to mean anyone of overseas parentage, or with a black skin. It is not uncommon to meet

teachers and members of the public to whom all Asian immigrants are the same, irrespective of their country of origin, and for whom there is no difference between India and the West Indies. It goes without saying that **teachers and others should have an informed and sympathetic understanding of the children's different origins, the cultures of their homes, and the very real link between some of their countries and Britain.** No one should accept a stereotype of 'the immigrant child', but should acknowledge the very great differences there are between children who fall into this general category. There are differences not only of language and culture, but in the manner in which families succeed or fail in settling here, and in providing a secure home for the children. Many immigrant children come from stable supportive families in which the relative affluence of the parents is evident; others face grave problems of insecurity and hardship, and in many respects resemble some of the indigenous families in the same inner city area.

20.4 ... the needs of the (immigrant) children who are already here are continuing ones. They cannot be dealt with briefly and then forgotten.

20.5 Immigrant children's attainment in tests and at school in general is related not only to language but to several other issues, particularly those of cultural identity and cultural knowledge. **No child should be expected to cast off the language and culture of the home as he crosses the school threshold, nor to live and act as though school and home represent two totally separate and different cultures which have to be kept firmly apart. The curriculum should reflect many elements of that part of his life which a child lives outside school ... many more schools in multiracial areas turn a blind eye to the fact that the community they serve has radically altered over the last ten years and is now one in which new cultures are represented. We see implications here for the education of all children, not just those of families of overseas origin.** One aspect of the question which we believe merits urgent attention is the nature of the reading material that is used in schools. In their verbal representation of society, and in their visual content, books do a great deal to shape children's attitudes. We would urge that **teachers and librarians should have this in mind when selecting books for schools.** If the school serves a multiracial society, does it have books about the homelands of its immigrant families, about their religions and cultures and their experiences in this country? ... Even more important, has the school removed from its shelves books which have a strong ethnocentric bias and contain outdated or insulting views of people of other cultures? ... **These and related questions should also enter the initial training of teachers, for whether or not they go to teach in schools with immigrant children it is right that they should have this kind of awareness.** This is an appropriate point to record our conclusion that there are not enough books available which represent children of overseas backgrounds in the ways we have been describing. **We address this observation to publishers, whose contribution in this whole area is potentially very considerable.**

20.12 ... **We were impressed by the efforts of schools we visited in Bolton and Bradford, where the specially appointed language specialists had devised a flexible cooperative system within the school. They functioned both as teachers and consultants, sitting in on subject classes, analysing the linguistic demands made on immigrant learners in different areas of the curriculum, and offering running help to the children as the class proceeded.** This is a much more effective way of working than dealing with pupils in comparative seclusion, which is bad both linguistically and socially ...

20.13 We have suggested that those authorities with areas of immigrant settlement should maintain a continuous assessment of the language needs of immigrant pupils in their schools ...

20.14 A special word needs to be added about children of overseas parentage in infant and nursery classes. In the first place we see the provision of nursery classes in inner city areas as having great importance for the early language development of immigrant children ...

20.15 Until now there has been a shortage of nursery provision in many of the areas where there are large numbers of overseas families. The promised expansion of nursery education will do something to remedy this, but there are two important points to be made. **First, it is clear that the conventional training of nursery and infant teachers has normally lacked a component that will help them understand the specific language difficulties and cultural values of children from families of overseas origin. There is a need for both these aspects to be taken into account in teacher-training programmes and in-service education. Secondly, new approaches may be necessary if these children are to be reached in their early years. The links of such families with the existing schools are often tenuous.** Mothers may be at work all day, or live in purdah, or speak no English; fathers may be permanently on night shift. Notices sent from school are sometimes not read, or are misinterpreted. The parents sometimes want to delegate to the school full responsibility for social training. In some instances they know nothing of the possibilities of nursery education and feel unable to take advantage of it where it exists. In the case of many of these families the conventional channels of communication between school and home do not function, and quite different strategies are needed.

20.16 There are good arguments for a more sustained and systematic service linking home and school, especially in the areas of intensive immigrant settlement. In some areas there is evidence of good results ensuing from various systems of home visiting ...

20.17 The importance of bilingualism, both in education and for society in general, has been increasingly recognised in Europe and in the USA. We believe that its implications for Britain should receive equally serious study. When bilingualism in Britain is discussed it is seldom if ever with reference to the inner city immigrant populations, yet over half the immigrant pupils in our schools have a mother tongue which is not English, and in some schools this means over 75% of the total number on roll. The language of the home and of a great deal of the central experience of their life is one of the Indian languages, or Greek, Turkish, Italian or Spanish. These children are genuine bilinguals, but this fact is often ignored or unrecognised by the schools. Their bilingualism is of great importance to the children and their families, and also to society as a whole. In a linguistically conscious nation in the modern world we should see it as an asset, as something to be nurtured, and one of the agencies which should nurture it is the school. Certainly the school should adopt a positive attitude to its pupils' bilingualism and wherever possible should help maintain and deepen their knowledge of their mother tongues. The school that really welcomes its immigrant parents must also be prepared to welcome their languages, to display notices and other materials written in them, and even to adopt some of the rhymes and songs learnt by the young children at home. . . . In any event, bilingual pupils should be encouraged to maintain their mother tongue throughout their schooling . . .

As you can see I have edited much of the report, put the key sections in bold and enlarged the last line above, which carries the same message as this book. And here, just for pleasure, is what I call Stuart Hall's cultural history.

I was born in Jamaica, and grew up in a middle-class family. My father spent most of his working life in the United Fruit Company. He was the first Jamaican to be promoted in every job he had; before him, those jobs were occupied by people sent down from the head office in America. What's important to understand is both the class fractions and the colour fractions from which my parents came. My father's and my mother's families were both middle-class but from very different class formations. [. . .]

My father belonged to the coloured lower-middle-class. His father kept a drugstore in a poor village in the country outside Kingston. The family was ethnically very mixed-African, East Indian, Portuguese, Jewish. My mother's family was much fairer in colour; indeed if you had seen her uncle, you would have thought he was an English expatriate, nearly white, or what we would call 'local white'. She was adopted by an aunt, whose sons – one a lawyer, one a doctor, trained in England. She was brought up in a beautiful house on the hill, above a small estate where the family lived. [. . .]

Culturally present in my own family was therefore this lower-middle-class, Jamaican, country manifestly dark skinned, and then this lighter-skinned English-oriented, plantation-oriented fraction, etc. [. . .]

So what was played out in my family, culturally, from the very beginning, was the conflict between the local and the imperial in the colonized context. Both these class fractions were opposed to the majority culture of poor Jamaican black people: highly race and colour conscious, and identifying with the colonizers. [...]

I was the blackest member of my family. The story in my family, which was always told as a joke, was that when I was born, my sister, who was much fairer than I, looked into the crib and she said, 'Where did you get this coolie baby from?' Now 'coolie' is the abusive word in Jamaica for a poor East Indian, who was considered the lowest of the low. So she wouldn't say 'Where did you get this black baby from?', since it was unthinkable that she could have a black brother. But she did notice that I was a different colour from her. This is very common in coloured middle-class Jamaican families, because they are the product of mixed liaisons between African slaves and European slave-masters, and the children then come out in varying shades. [...]

So I always had the identity in my family of being the one from the outside, the one who didn't fit, the one who was blacker than the others, 'the little coolie', etc. And I performed that role throughout. My friends at school, many of whom were from good middle-class homes, but blacker in colour than me, were not accepted at my home. My parents didn't think I was making the right kind of friends. They always encouraged me to mix with more middle-class, more higher-colour, friends, and I didn't. Instead, I withdrew emotionally from my family and met my friends elsewhere. My adolescence was spent continuously negotiating these cultural spaces.

(Chen, 1996: 486–505)

What we learn from this

We learn the importance of looking beyond the apparent surface meaning and of reading more carefully and critically.

Section III

Supporting children in classes and settings to learn and remain attached to their languages and cultures

> 'Bilingualism is not like a bicycle with two balanced wheels, but more like an all-terrain vehicle'
>
> (Ofelia Garcia, 2009a)

In this third section of the book we move to thinking about how educators must and can support the learning of all children, taking special account of the needs of bilingual learners. The term special needs is used here to mean individual needs: there is no suggestion that bilingual children have 'special needs' in the conventional meaning of that phrase. Essentially this chapter has a focus on *pedagogy* and we examine these issues:

- The importance of knowing as much as possible about the children you are working with or are interested in.
- Understanding bilingual children's use of translanguaging (or code-switching) and multimodality (or modes or ways of communication using textual, aural, linguistic, spatial and visual resources) in their play, linguistic development and learning.
- Celebrating and supporting bilingual learners through appropriate pedagogy and establishing and maintaining effective links with all homes and particularly those where the first language is one other than English.

By now you all know that children hear and acquire language/s from infancy through their everyday interactions in the daily routines or formats of their homes – at meal times, bedtime, when clearing up, playing, out for a walk, having an argument, throwing a tantrum – all moments of learning and language. They hear how experienced users of the language or languages do things and make things happen with language. These small children are effectively *apprentices in the everyday world of their languages*. Wherever language is used, the situation and the language are rule-bound and goal seeking, and induct the child into the rules or conventions or rituals and values of the home, the community, the culture. The rules may be bent or broken but by listening and watching, mimicking and practising, transforming and absorbing the ways in which words are used in all the available sites and situations of daily life the young child begins to join her *first community of language users*. She is a *meaning maker* and a *meaning sharer* who is learning when to be silent, what to talk about and when and to whom, how to take turns in conversation, who has more power in talk or to use gesture and other aspects of communication.

You read earlier about how children acquiring their mother tongue work out the rules that bind their language together. They can then either keep to the rules or try changing them to see what happens. You should be alert to noticing if children are paying attention to the patterns they experience in their lives and how they use these to make, discover, use and invent rules. If you are engaging with the child you can scaffold their learning through interactions, responses, sharing gaze, repeating sounds and more. It is a question of looking, listening and analysing. It was Jerome Bruner who drew attention to the importance of daily routines in the lives of young children. Think about how the primary caregiver – often, but not always, the mother – interacts with the child at bath time, meal times, bedtime, nappy-change time. The adult often cues the child's response. She might tickle the baby as she changes her nappy, or clap her hands when the baby holds the spoon. The baby does something, the mother responds verbally or physically; the baby 'answers back'. It is like a turn-taking dance. And this takes place in whatever language is the language of mother and baby.

The young bilingual child has been engaging in these exchanges with the people who love and care for and talk to her in her mother tongue. And then she moves away from home to go to a nursery class or a creche or a school where she might find that no one understands what she is saying and she understands nothing people say to her. Put yourself in her shoes if you can and consider what might help this be less lonely and alienating.

Chapter 8

Making sense of a new world

All children who come into the nursery or setting have already had consider-able experience of and competence in being language users. This applies to all the languages the child has been exposed to. They can all 'read' social situations and contribute to them by talking themselves, listening, joining in, commenting on, smiling at and laughing with. Bilingual children, moving away from home and into a nursery or playgroup, class or setting truly have to make sense of a new world. It is a world made up of people they don't yet know, who they might not understand and who might not understand them, and they are asked to do things that have few, if any, links with their prior experience. How can this daunting task be made easier?

Drury (2007) tells us that children's communication with adults in the nursery will usually be shaped by the cultural expectations and values typical of an English approach to school and early education and that, almost always, will involve particular ways of talking and interacting that some of the children may not be familiar with. Such communicative mismatches often pose considerable challenges for these children, who may find themselves in the double-bind situation of having to achieve academic success in a language and environment they do not yet understand. Rose Drury captures some of this in her account of Pahari speaking Nazma:

> Nazma enters nursery holding her sister's hand. Her sister, Yasmin (aged 4½), moves over to the large carpet where the children sit with the nursery teacher at the beginning of every session. Nazma follows her, chewing her dress, staying close to her sister and watching everything. She had stopped crying during the fifth week at nursery and she now comes every afternoon. The children listen to the teacher talking about caterpillars and many join in the discussion in English. Nazma is silent. Mussarat, the Bilingual Teaching Assistant (BTA), enters the nursery. She gathers a small group of Pahari speaking children together to share a book. This activity had been planned with the nursery teacher and linked to the current topic. The children switch to Pahari (their mother tongue) for this activity. Nazma listens and points

to a picture of a dog (kutha) and cat (billee) in an Urdu alphabet picture book, but does not speak. They go outside to play. Nazma stands on the outside watching the other children and holds Mussarat's hand. She has learned the climbing frame routine and repeats the climbing and sliding activity several times. The children go inside and choose from a range of play activities. Nazma watches. She stays at an activity for one minute and moves on. This is repeated several times. Then she wanders around the room sucking her fingers. It is now story time on the carpet. The children sit and listen to the story *The Very Hungry Caterpillar*. Nazma sits close to her sister and watches. Their mother appears at the door and they go home.

(Drury, 2007: 31)

How would you say that Nazma 'reads' the situation of being in the nursery? Is she able to join in and communicate? Can she share her languages in a meaningful way? Now read the next extract where you find Nazma working in a small group of children with Mussarat, the bilingual classroom assistant who is telling the story of *The Very Hungry Caterpillar* in Pahari.

Nazma: we eat it at home [pointing to picture of water melon in book] we eat it [excitedly]
[Nazma joins in counting the fruit in the book – in English]
Mussarat: he was a beautiful butterfly
Nazma: I've seen a butterfly in my garden
Mussarat: how many eyes?
Nazma: two eyes … One came in my garden

(Drury, 2007: 76)

This is how Drury analyses this:

This excerpt shows Nazma at her most responsive in nursery. Unlike any other interaction in this context, she is able to contribute her personal experience to the story telling session with the BTA [bilingual teaching assistant].

(Drury, 2013: 389)

How would you evaluate Nazma's spontaneous response to the picture of the butterfly at the end of the story? Did you notice how she was able to relate this to her own experience of butterflies in her garden? In this example we find both the importance of a child being able to draw on previous experience and of a child having direct access to meaning, provided here by Mussarat, the mediator of culture and language for Nazma. It is important to know that during Nazma's early days of schooling she only spoke when Mussarat was there. This little girl found the transition from home very difficult, as many children do. The language of Pahari was the basis for Nazma's early cognitive and linguistic development. It was her mother tongue and so the language in which she thought and talked about her life, her feelings, her relationships. On entering the school she would at some stage have to come to understand and use English, but had she not had Mussarat there it would have been doubly difficult for her.

> For Nazma, without Pahari, and the opportunity to use it with a mediator, she would be a wholly isolated individual in a context where only English is spoken. Her mother tongue represents an ongoing bond between home and school, and thus an important continuity between the two domains. The tension for Nazma is to make the adjustment from home to school without losing the language and culture that sustain her.
>
> (Drury, 2013: 390)

As young children acquire a second language their competence is *diglossic* in the sense that they are able to shift the style and type of language they use to match the people and situation involved. Rosa Ochoa (in her language history) told us that her first son, Miguel, was 6 months old when they went to Australia and at that time she writes that she

> spoke to him in Spanish, my husband spoke to him in English and my husband's family spoke to him in Italian and Calabrese. . . . I did a little study of his language learning as part of my Masters in linguistics (code switching) and it was very interesting to see how he knew who to talk to in what language. Never made a mistake and occasionally would code switch within a sentence and use all four languages without making any grammatical errors.

Learning your first language or languages is a considerable cognitive achievement, perhaps more so in light of the fact that no formal teaching of the grammar, vocabulary, structure, rules and conventions of the language is given. Rather the learning takes place socially, through interactions with more expert others, in diverse situations or contexts. Everyone seems to applaud and celebrate this when the language is one that is highly regarded (like English or French or Latin): sadly, where the language is other than one of these, the speaker may be regarded as, in some way, being incomplete. Learning to adapt to the school or setting, with its own culture, particular rules and practices, is difficult enough without the added difficulty of not understanding the language of learning. In some schools and settings children have to put up a hand in order to be able to talk. Where else are questions asked where only one answer is the 'correct' one? So the young bilingual child is faced not only with a new language but also with a whole set of new rules and regulations, conventions and behaviours to negotiate.

Cummins studied and considered very carefully just what happens to young children acquiring and using two languages. In his analysis he considered both the *cognitive difficulty* of the task facing the young bilingual learner and how *meaningful the task is to the child in terms of context*. For very young children the *context* is what determines how meaningful any task is. You may be familiar with the work of Margaret Donaldson (1978), who said that young children find it easier to solve problems when the task makes *human sense* to them. Making human sense means being able to see the point or the purpose of the task. So for young children the *concrete* (which means dealing with real things in meaningful contexts where the child can make sense of the problem) must come before the *abstract*. It is for this reason that good early years provision ensures a great deal of first hand exploration. In good nurseries and other settings you are likely to find activities like planting and growing things, cooking and baking, bathing and dressing the dolls, making marks on paper, setting up a clinic, laying the tables for lunch – all of which are full of possibilities for children to explore their world drawing on their previous experience. The key phrase to keep in mind is '*being able to make sense of something by drawing on your previous experience*'. Good practitioners talk of helping young children by trying to ensure that most of the things that they encounter in settings and classrooms are things that both make human sense to the children and allow them to draw on previous experience. A question you might like to ask is whether completing a worksheet, colouring in a picture, or chanting the sounds individual letters make can be described as being meaningful contexts.

In his early work in the mid-1980s, Cummins invented and examined the relationship between two terms: *Basic Interpersonal Communicative Skills* (BICS), which means the development of conversational fluency in a second language; and *Cognitive Academic Language Proficiency* (CALP), which describes the use of language in decontextualised academic situations. In short, BICS is the spoken language we use in our everyday lives and CALP is the spoken language we use when we consider academic and abstract things. Cummins used a simple matrix or diagram to illustrate the relationship between the two (see Figure 8.1). In this matrix the horizontal axis represents a continuum from *context embedded* (which we might say makes human sense to the learner) to *context reduced* (which is more abstract). There is a continuum from where the learner can use external clues and information, such as facial expression, gestures, real objects and pictorial representation to help understanding, to the other extreme where there is no helpful context. The vertical axis relates to the extent of cognitive involvement or difficulty of a task, moving from those that are not very demanding to those that are increasingly challenging.

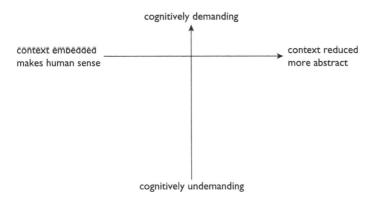

Figure 8.1 The significance of context-embedded activities for young bilingual learners

Below you will find a drawing and here is a task for you to do. Where on this continuum would you put the question 'Where is the house with the pointed roof?' Are there clues you can use so that it is context embedded or not?

If you had asked a young child this question she could easily use the context (which is the picture) to point to the only building in the picture with a pointed roof. The picture holds enough information to make the task not very difficult or cognitively challenging and it is context embedded. I would place it in the lower left corner of the diagram.

Figure 8.2 Drawing by Hannah Gardiner used to illustrate the significance of offering context embedded activities for young bilingual learners

You will not be surprised to find that this is where many of the young bilingual learners will be in their development. Now, still thinking about context and how meaningful it is to a young child, consider a task common in many early years classes and settings where children are asked to colour all the big circles red and all the little circles blue. There may be a context, and the task is not cognitively demanding, but do ask what any reasonable child might ask: Why? Is there a valid reason for doing this? Is this a meaningful or context bound task? Yet you might well recognise this as one of the many meaningless tasks children are asked to do.

The message for educators is clear. Where you are preparing for newly arrived bilingual learners you will want to start with contextualised tasks and practical activities. After some time and with experience of, exposure to, support with and growing confidence in their languages, children may still need contextual support but will start to be able to deal with more cognitively demanding tasks. You can read more about this in Cline and Frederickson (1996). Cummins and other researchers suggest that it takes learners, on average, approximately 2 years to achieve a functional, social use of a second language but that it might take between 5 and 7 years or longer for some bilingual learners to achieve a level of what might be described as *academic linguistic proficiency* comparable to that of monolingual English speaking peers.

In his later work, Cummins (1984 and 2000) developed his ideas for what he called '*a common underlying proficiency*', also known as (CUP) or the *interdependence hypothesis*. In essence, what he was saying is that the second language and first or primary language have a shared foundation so that competence in the first or primary language provides the basis for competence in the second language. He believed that what a child has learned about and through a first or primary language will help learn a second language. The *Common Underlying Proficiency* refers to the *interdependence of concepts, skills and linguistic knowledge* found in a central processing system – the brain. Cummins famously used the analogy of an iceberg that has peaks above the waterline, one peak representing the surface features of the first language (namely the vocabulary and grammar) and another peak representing the surface features of the second language.

The diagram illustrating this was originally drawn by my granddaughter Hannah when she was a very little girl and appeared in my first book on this subject. I have added the brain and the labels. Below the waterline, unseen and unheard, is where the central operating system is located. It controls both languages. Have a go at answering this question: *If above the water are things like speaking, reading and writing, what would you guess lies below the waterline?* You will find the answer in the diagram on page 75.

The two peaks represent the child's two languages. The water line shows the boundary between the child's brain capacity and the outside world. What lies below the waterline is the brain and cognition.

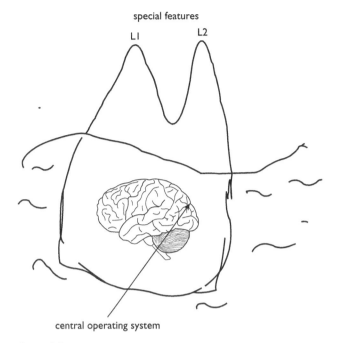

special features

central operating system

Figure 8.3

Cummins reminds us that knowledge and understanding of one language link to knowledge and understanding of new languages and that this is especially significant in relation to reading and writing. To illustrate this, Jean Conteh (2012) offers us a wonderful example of 9-year-old Mushtaq recently arrived from Bangladesh and not speaking English at all.

> He was sent to Conteh's language group on his first day where the group were working on story based activities. He was totally silent as they listened to an African story about the sun and moon. But the following day he brought to school a piece of paper covered in neat script. It was the story of the sun and moon written in Bengali. It turned out that another child in the class had told Mushtaq the story and he had used his knowledge of Bengali to write it out. He was clearly very literate in his mother tongue.
>
> (Conteh, 2012: 43)

In the diagram used by Cummins (like the one above) the two languages are outwardly distinct but are supported by shared concepts and knowledge derived from learning and experience and the cognitive and linguistic abilities of the learner. Cummins suggests this may also illustrate how linguistic knowledge is stored in the brain. We can think of bilingual speakers as having separately stored proficiencies or abilities in each language, which may include aspects of language like pronunciation, vocabulary and grammar. These might be stored in the working memory, which, in turn, has access to long-term memory storage that is not language specific. In other words, the use of the first or second language is informed by the working memory, but the concepts are stored as an underlying proficiency.

Cummins, like Chomsky, talked of surface and deeper level thinking skills. The deeper levels of thought and language – what we might call *higher order cognitive functions* – involve processes like analysis, synthesis and evaluation, which are all necessary to academic progress. Cummins distinguished these from more explicit or superficial realisations of linguistic and cognitive processing. He proposed that a minimum threshold of first language cognitive/academic development was necessary for success in second language learning. He also suggested that if the threshold of cognitive proficiency is not achieved, the learner may have difficulties in achieving bilingual proficiency – the ability to be fluent and articulate in both languages for many purposes.

This representation of bilingual proficiency would also suggest that continued conceptual and linguistic development in the first language would help second language learners in their learning of the second language. So continued support of the first language whilst learning the second language will be beneficial for cognitive development as well as for allowing the learner to retain her social and cultural links. In his later work, Cummins continued to cite the work of many other researchers that supports both this hypothesis and the claim that bilingualism and continued development in the first language enhance metalinguistic skills and development in proficiency in the second language.

What we learn from this

If we are considering how to ease young bilingual learners into this strange and lonely world there is a set of things we might consider:

- Understand the importance of *knowing as much as possible about each child, her languages, family background, prior experiences and culture.* In many settings and schools paying *a home visit* is common – although I have some misgivings about how this is done by the practitioners and how it is viewed by parents and carers. Gathering information that may be sensitive requires careful handling. Birgit Voss, who worked in Islington some years ago, wrote a piece for one of my books (Smidt, 2010), which I go on reproducing whenever I can. Here is what she said about her school's way of getting important information about the child prior to starting school. I have made some minimal changes to the text:

A record is usually started at the home visit. It is an adapted version of the Primary Learning Record which was developed during the days of the Inner London Education Authority (ILEA) ... parents help me to fill in the first page. It is our policy that each child gets this opportunity to meet me in the safety of her/his home environment. Last term, because of our continuous cuts in funding, the head teacher had to cover for my visits – an indication of how important we think this first home school link is. This term the Section 11 teacher [another ILEA feature: a teacher dedicated to the support of children with particular needs] will cover for my visits. I usually take a puzzle, a book, some drawing material and a photo book with pictures of the team, the school, our class and the children at work. We look through this book together, often with grandparents, aunts and uncles, as well as parents and the child and siblings. I chat a bit about the kind of things children can do in our class. The pictures speak for themselves when I am unable to communicate in the family's language. That, and a great deal of body language, smiles, gestures usually get the message across. During the visit, I also take some photographs of the child. They are used later when the child comes to school to mark her/his space on the coat hooks, the towel hook and the third, whole body one, for the magnet board. The home visit is a good opportunity to ask the parents to write their child's name in the family's language. I usually let them write it into the record. From there I can enlarge it on the photocopier at school and use it in our graphics area and anywhere else where the child's name appears in English. A very easy way to get dual language writing samples!

(Adapted from Voss, 2010: 61)

Birgit, bilingual herself, has a deeply personal as well as analytical approach to the needs of bilingual children and their families.

- Make evident that you *value the languages of the children's homes*. You can do this by reflecting aspects of them in the room but be careful to avoid tokenism. Do you have examples of the scripts used in the home languages of the children on display? You can buy these online or ask parents and other family members to write them for you. Do you have a selection of classroom books for you to read and children to look through? Having books in the languages of the children is so important and will draw you into other cultures. They may well reflect something that all children can relate to. You can make your own dual text books with the help of parents and others who speak the community languages in your setting.

- Ensure that *the curriculum is soundly based on contexts and situations that make human sense* to the children, so that they can build on their previous experience and work towards the abstract. Avoid spending time and energy on worksheets and closed activities. Set up your room so that it is inviting to all the children.

- Ensure that you make it clear to the children and their families that the *language and literacies of home are valued and welcomed* in the classroom or setting.
- Remember that young children *first encounter literacy – reading and writing – in their homes*. What is read and written in their homes will be different from what is read in your home or mine. But whatever it is, it is laying the foundations for the children to become effective communicators. Manjula Datta (2000), a multilingual educator and writer, says this about her early language learning:

> I didn't go to school until I was 7. My mother taught me, along with my brothers and sisters, to read and write in Bengali, Hindi and English at home, almost simultaneously. Looking back on it, it was not an insurmountable task for my mother, nor were we prodigious children. How did I learn to be literate in three languages at the same time?... My mother taught me to decode text in Bengali very early using phonic skills. I was already a competent speaker of Bengali. I was able to operate on the semantic and syntactic level with comparative ease. Reading in Bengali made sense to me. My literacy development in Hindi was interesting, linguistically speaking. It demonstrated how knowledge and skills are transferable between languages. Bengali and Hindi share a common lexis and syntax, although there are some differences in script, pronunciation and the use of the operative verb ... learning to read in English (which was my third language at this stage) may appear quite simple at one level. Learning the alphabet followed a singsong pattern and was accompanied by vowel practice – for example, the cat sat on the mat – to decode simple words. My mother used the same method of teaching me the graphophonic principles in English as she had in Bengali and Hindi.
>
> (Datta, 2000: 35)

As a monolingual adult I find this child's home experience of language and literacy enviable; the reality is that Mandula's linguistic history is shared by thousands of young bilinguals. Imagine their feelings when their languages are not shared and often looked down on.

- Remember that there is a positive effect on the bilingual learner's identity, self-esteem and confidence when she is treated as having as much to offer as monolingual children and her language and her linguistic capacity are recognised and respected. Draw attention to diversity and celebrate it. One way to do this is to get the children themselves to demonstrate to their peers what they know that others don't.

Chapter 9

Understanding multimodality and translanguaging in early education

Bilingual children do not always keep their two or more languages separate. They switch and mix as they talk. This used to be called code-switching but that has been replaced by the rather clumsy word translanguaging, which was a term first used as a Welsh word in schools in Wales in the 1980s, particularly by Cen Williams in a report to the Welsh Assembly (1994), where it was defined like this:

2.3 Translanguaging – a skill for developing bilingualism

Translanguaging simply means (i) receiving information in one language and (ii) using or applying it in the other language. It is a skill that happens naturally in everyday life, e.g. when a child receives a telephone message for his/her mother in English and conveys the message to her in Welsh. This skill needs to be developed systematically throughout the Education system so that pupils are able to switch efficiently from one language to the other, thus fully utilising their bilingual capability.

(Williams, 1994)

This definition of translanguaging was adopted and made popular through two books: Baker's *Foundations of Bilingual Education and Bilingualism* (in all five editions) and Ofelia Garcia's (2009a) *Bilingual Education in the 21st Century*. A precise definition of the term is difficult but it is generally used to describe what happens when a bilingual speaker uses both or all of her languages, in one utterance, as part of the process of making meaning, shaping experiences, gaining understanding and knowledge. It is code-switching in another guise. The word code-switching was often used to indicate a child's fallibility as a language learner. Researchers such as Garcia (2009a) and Blackledge and Creese (2010), amongst others, note that translanguage is in fact a way in which both languages are used in a dynamic and functionally integrated manner to organise and mediate mental processes in understanding, speaking and literacy learning. You will find examples of this in the language histories together with the responses of others to children translanguaging. In simple terms, what is happening is that the child, eager to communicate, uses the vocabulary and grammar of the language that best allow her to communicate at that point in time. Responding positively to this is important because even very young children pick up messages about how their language or languages are perceived by others. How their use of language is judged also affects children's sense of self. It does not take long for a child to recognise that her language is perhaps seen as having no place in the school or setting and that being bilingual has no value.

Multimodality is what we often see in young children as they use several semiotic modes or different signs and symbols in order to make something meaningful to them. When used in connection with verbal communication (i.e. words) it means all the things that help the speaker make her intentions or ideas clear. She might use particular accents, tones of voice, real or made-up words or phrases or, indeed, languages; ask questions, make demands, narrate, use sub-intentional hand movements, gesture, facial expression and more.

François Grosjean wrote a book in 1982 called *Life with Two Languages: An Introduction to Bilingualism,* in which he offered evidence that code-switching in bilingual children is common and not evidence of any cognitive confusion or lack of comprehension. Rather, children select words or phrases according to who they are talking to, what they are talking about, what each language means to them and more. He encapsulated this perfectly in a later work where he said that a bilingual person is not the sum of two monolinguals any more than a hurdler is the sum of a sprinter and a high jumper (Grosjean, 1985). Garcia (2009a) put this differently but just as cogently. She said that bilingualism is '*not monolingualism times two*' (2009a: 71), '*not like a bicycle with two balanced wheels*' but '*more like an all-terrain vehicle*' whose wheels '*extend and contract, flex and stretch, making possible, over highly uneven ground, movement forward that is bumpy and irregular but also sustained and effective*' (2009a: 45). This analogy pleases me because it shows just how complicated the task facing the bilingual child using two language is. She went on to say: '*Regardless of how children come to be bilingual or multilingual, children throughout the world commonly engage in bilingual languishing or what I have termed elsewhere, translanguaging*' (Garcia, 2009b).

Bilingual languishing! What an amazing thought. If we think of translanguaging as the act performed by bilinguals of accessing different features of various modes of what are described as autonomous languages, in order to maximise communicative potential, we get a sense of how intentional and impressive it is. It implies an approach to bilingualism that is centred, not on languages as has often been the case, but on the practices of bilinguals – what they do – in order to make sense of their multilingual worlds. Therefore, translanguaging goes beyond what has been termed code-switching, although it does include it.

Mileidis Gort and Ryan Pontier (2012) carried out some research on the use and function of translanguage in Miami and coined the phrase 'sheltered instruction', which, they say, is

> an approach in which teachers modify and mediate instruction to make language and content comprehensible to students learning in a second language. Developed to support sustained periods of monolingual instruction, sheltering requires that teachers use a combination of strategies to facilitate student understanding without resorting to translation.
>
> (Gort & Pontier, 2012: 3)

The place of translanguaging is not apparent but much in this piece is worth looking at more closely and more critically. We will attempt to evaluate the efficacy of Gort and Pontier's pedagogy. They state that in the case where there are children defined as emergent bilinguals, their teachers can make input comprehensible in the early stages of second language acquisition by using various linguistic and paralinguistic strategies, such as speaking more slowly, enunciating more clearly, repeating words or phrases and using gesture and other aids to assist meaning. The study took place in two preschool classrooms within a setting operating what Gort and Pontier called an additive Spanish/English dual language (DL) preschool programme in a multilingual and multicultural community in the southeastern United States. One of the preschool's primary goals was to expose children to authentic experiences in each of the target languages, Spanish and English. Do look out for evidence of what you feel might constitute authentic experiences. This, on the surface, appears to be a laudable aim. There were approximately 130 children in the school aged 6 weeks to 5 years old, coming from a range of cultural, linguistic and socioeconomic backgrounds. Two teachers were assigned to each preschool classroom. At the time of the study, the DL preschool programme followed what Gort and Pontier termed a 'language policy of separation' (i.e. parallel/dual monolingualism) through which teachers were encouraged to model monolingual use of each target language and discouraged from moving between, or mixing, languages. So translanguage was positively discouraged. In the two preschool classrooms, the two teacher pairs applied the language separation policy in different ways.

> In one classroom, the two target languages were distributed by time (i.e., morning/afternoon) so that both teachers spoke English in the morning and Spanish in the afternoon when leading whole group activities and interacting with children individually and in small group settings. This approach to language separation created a (generally) monolingual instructional language context wherein the same language was used by both teachers during specific times of the day; however, because both

teachers actively used each target language for instruction and in social interaction with the children and each other at designated times of the day, they served as bilingual models of the program's target languages (albeit ones who kept their languages [mostly] separate).

The teachers in the second classroom adopted a 'one-teacher/one-language' approach, so that one teacher served as the Spanish language model and the other served as the English language model at all times. Each teacher in this classroom took turns leading large group activities as the target language of large group instruction alternated on a weekly basis. This meant that the Spanish-model teacher led large group activities during alternating 'Spanish' weeks, and vice-versa. In small groups and individual interactions, each teacher used her designated language throughout the day to communicate with children and each other. This approach to language separation created a bilingual instructional language context, wherein both languages were used concurrently throughout the day as both teachers were generally present and involved in small and large group activities, albeit to different degrees. In this classroom, each teacher served as a monolingual model of one of the DL program's target languages (although both teachers demonstrated receptive bilingual skills when interacting with students and colleagues who addressed them in their non-designated language).

(Gort & Pontier, 2012: 5–6)

I have some difficulty thinking about the suitability of large group activities for the babies – remember they take children from the age of 6 weeks – and their plan is so complicated that it gives me brain ache. They say that a bilingual pedagogy requires much more than teachers or children merely fixing their languages or translanguaging. It needs educators to use a range of discursive practices that invite bilingual children to engage in activities, events and dialogues and exchanges in order to make sense of their bilingual worlds. Educators need to design spaces and activities where language use is fostered and make these as like real-life situations as they can so that the interactions and dialogues that take place allow the children to draw on their prior and out of school/settings lives. Gort and Pontier (2012) say:

Our findings corroborate previous research that suggests that a strict language separation approach, as traditionally implemented in DL programs, may be at odds with the natural social interactions of bilinguals, who typically draw on a number of communicative strategies, including translanguaging, to construct meaning.... [And our] findings support the notion that the integration of two languages can be a useful pedagogic practice in promoting the DL development of emergent bilinguals.

(Gort & Pontier, 2012: 18)

Kenner (2004a) and Sneddon (2000) have both shown, in their research, that bilingual children do not see their languages or their literacies, as they acquire them, as separate, but rather as being simultaneous. Here are some ideas from the early work of Kenner as she looked at young bilingual children considering their own early writing and that of their peers. She noticed that children use more than one language not only when speaking but also when beginning to explore the conventions of more than one written language system. So just as these children live their daily lives in more than one spoken language, so the children in the study revealed that they had more than one system for written representation always available to them. They could draw on either or both systems when writing, sometimes choosing to combine both in one text. In some cases, this involved transferring from one system to the other as they wrote, while in other examples children's experience of *simultaneity* operated to such a degree that both written languages appeared within a single word.

Kenner says that 'simultaneity' of experience should not be equated with 'confusion'. Bilingual children are far from confused. They know that they are operating with two or more systems. And when writing they can offer a reason for the choice of sign or symbol used. All of this is powerful evidence of the brilliance of young children.

Here is what Kenner (2004b) tells us about one child's choices.

Tala was determined to make the English and Arabic alphabets map onto each other. She was observed at home, engaged in this project which was entirely of her own devising. On one occasion, having written the English alphabet sequence, she then started writing letters from the Arabic alphabet sequence directly above each English letter. On another occasion, she began with the Arabic alphabet and tried to map the English letter sequence 'A, B . . .' onto it. Both alphabets do indeed start with letters which represent near-equivalent sounds (/a/ and /b/), but after that the elements only match occasionally. However, whilst recognising these disparities, Tala was not to be deterred. An additional opportunity to pursue her aim arose in a peer teaching session. One of Tala's classmates adopted the strategy of interpreting a new script by using the already known English system (a common strategy discussed above) saying 'A, B, C, D . . .' and so on as she pointed to letters on an Arabic alphabet chart whilst moving her finger across each line from left to right. Tala joined in with this activity, because although she was aware that two different systems were involved, it connected with her own aim of identifying specific links between the alphabets.

The two girls were looking particularly for the letter 'T', chosen as significant because it was the first letter of both their names. Tala showed where you would expect to find the letter 'T' if reciting the English alphabet, and following the Arabic alphabet grid from left to right, and then if reciting the English alphabet and following the grid from right to left with Arabic directionality. Neither of these positions actually yielded the Arabic /t/, the correct position of which Tala had previously identified. However, Tala continued to try to implement her desired linkages by explaining 'Some of Arabic and English look similar to each other, of the letters' and showing how one particular Arabic alphabet symbol 'looks similar to T only if you chop that off' (indicating the detail which would need to be removed) 'and put a line here' (indicating what would need to be added).

The result would indeed have been an English 'T'.

(Kenner, 2004b: 56)

I find this – and much else in Kenner's work – fascinating. It interests me as much for revealing the cognitive achievements of the children as for the ability of this researcher to *observe and analyse so closely*. She is renowned for her work on young children learning about languages and writing through peer teaching. Here is an extract from a piece she wrote for a book I edited in 2010. She is analysing how a young bilingual child, Ming, taught his classmates how to write in his mother tongue Chinese. In preparing to understand what Ming was doing, Kenner had to do what the children do when they begin to learn to write in English or any other language, which is to pay careful attention to how one symbol looks different from another. Chinese symbols are complex and meaning can be conveyed by small differences between them. Children learning Chinese have a head start in developing visual discrimination skills, and they can encourage their English school classmates to look closely at writing as well. Kenner's introduction to the piece suggests just how much research into a specific language she has had to do to be able to interpret what the child, as teacher, is saying and doing.

Each Chinese character is built up from a pattern of strokes, which children have to learn to recognise. A small difference in the stroke pattern can make the character look like another one with a different meaning. Children must notice how long each stroke is, what angle it is placed at and whether it is straight or curved. [...]

One day Ming taught his Year 1 primary school class how to write in Chinese. Each child used a small whiteboard, as they often did for literacy lessons in English. Following Ming's example, they tried to copy the character for 'ten', which looks like a plus sign in English. Ming inspected the results and gave his opinion, saying, for example, 'it looks neat' or 'it's wonky and it's not straight'. Children began to realise that Chinese was not as easy as they had thought. They made greater efforts to get their lines straighter and the right length.

(Kenner, in Smidt, 2010: 67)

Jennifer Miller (2003) carried out research into the aspects of the world that a young bilingual child has to negotiate in order to be *properly heard and accepted* into the host group. This could involve knowing what accent to use, whether to look the speaker in the eyes, whether to speak softly or loudly, or what form of address to use. Many of us have been in situations where we are unsure of what would be regarded as inappropriate in interaction. It is important to remember that rules and conventions can change as society changes. Marion Iacopucci still reacts angrily when addressed by the informal 'tu' by anyone younger than she is. I am baffled by this because the rules of polite talk are less rigid here than they still are in Italy. Mary Bucholtz (2003) called these conventions 'the norms' and said that are often being explored by the bilingual child trying to get acceptance and recognition from the 'insider' group. In other words the child seeks *authentication* – to be admitted to some accepted group. This is close to the ideas of Pierre Bourdieu (1977), who talked of such things as the '*right to speech*' and '*the power to impose reception*'. He used the terms *social capital* and *cultural capital*. Cultural capital is, loosely, the way you speak, the place where you live, the work your parents do, the books you read, the kind of music you appreciate. This cultural capital defines which social group you are a member of. Social capital is the connections you have to others in a defined group. There is also *symbolic capital*, which refers to things like fame, prestige and reputation. Cultural capital will vary from culture to culture.

> When my oldest granddaughter went to South Africa as a small child she spoke only English, which made her different from most of the children she encountered in her first nursery school in South Africa. As the first of her generation in our family she received a great deal of attention from all the adults, and this attention was largely focused around narrative, story, songs and books. For some time she struggled to be admitted to the group because her experience had been so different from theirs. At nursery she spent time being very quiet but watching intently and listening hard and it was only after a holiday, during which she watched a film of The Secret Garden on TV with her family one day when it rained, that she began to use what was at hand to explore her feelings. She was entranced by the story, clearly making some links to Mary – the morose little girl who is a newcomer to the place where the story is set. Using a set of plastic dinosaurs she played out, day after day, scenes from the film in her own explorations and elaborations. On her return to the nursery after her holiday she took the dinosaurs into the nursery class and gradually these proved the key to her authentication. What intrigued me was how what seemed to be the key feature for her was the colour of the dinosaurs: Mary was always pink, Dickon was always purple and the horse was always black.
>
> (based on Smidt, 2001: 26)

Multimodality is a relatively new term but the act of using different modes to express ideas and feelings is as old as culture. Language was traditionally the focus for the evaluation and development of young children's learning. A multimodal perspective broadens that view, allowing us to see learning as involving more than words. The significance of this for bilingual children is obvious. They may have the words but cannot yet share them with their peers and adults in the class or setting. Multimodal approaches to communication and meaning making take into account the whole range of 'modes' or ways of expression. In other words it allows for all the 'languages' that young children encounter in their lives at home, in the community, on tablets, on TV, at the park, in the shops and more. The range and combinations of modes they use to make and express meaning can involve gesture, movement, gaze, facial expression, image, music, sound effects and language. Thus multimodality offers a fundamentally different perspective on communication in that it does not assume that language always plays the central role in all interactions. This change in perspective can offer radically new insights into understanding communicative and learning processes – particularly in the current era where digital technologies have fundamentally changed the kinds of representational tools and modes that are used in knowledge construction and exchange. This is true for us: meaning making and meaning sharing in multilingual classes and settings need to be scrutinised for the meaning in what might seem random.

Gunther Kress has written a great deal about how young children use what is at hand to create something that is deeply meaningful to them, and share this with others. He says that children act multimodally in the things that they choose, the objects or artefacts that they make and how they use their bodies. He was particularly interested in young children learning to become literate and looked at their early attempts to share their thoughts in 'writing'. In one example two little girls, each aged 3 plus years, one from an English family and the other from a Taiwanese family, each gave Kress a sample of their writing and in each one he noticed the impact of their culture on what they were doing. Both had clearly seen things written in their home languages. Both were creative and transformative. What they produced was not necessarily meaningful to others, but each was unique and clearly influenced by the shapes of scripts they had encountered in their home lives. And yet they were not direct copies of anything. Kress says, '*in working with these already shaped objects, children, like all makers of signs, are constantly innovative, creative, transformative*' (1997: 61).

Kress, with his particular interest in literacy, is much to be admired and his work is very readable. He had no particular interest in bilingualism but his ideas on ways into literacy seem to work for ways into communication per se. What is at hand – or freely available in any environment – will be used by children to create something new and unique. It is worth remembering this in terms of what you offer in your classroom or setting.

Multimodality is an inter-disciplinary approach that understands communication and representation to be about more than language. This is where its importance for us lies. There are three interconnected theoretical assumptions that underpin multimodality:

1 Multimodality assumes that representation and communication always draw on what is called a '*multiplicity of modes*', all of which contribute to meaning. It focuses on analysing and describing the full repertoire of meaning-making resources that people use in different contexts and that may be visual, spoken, gestural, written, three-dimensional and others, depending on the domain or type of representation. In addition to considering the range of meaning-making devices it also analyses how these are organised in order to both make and share meanings.

2 It assumes that resources are socially and culturally shaped over time to become meaning-making resources that articulate the different cultural, social and individual ways of doing things within different communities. In South Africa, children make human figures out of nuts or clay; of fabric, of wire, of recycled tin cans and plastic bags. They make wheeled toys out of wire; musical instruments out of coconut shells and seed pods; jewellery out of stones and shells and wire.

3 People make meaning through their selection and configuration of modes of representation. Dance in India may well differ from that in Nepal: the scripts of Arabic and Hebrew are very different.

What we learn from this

Educators will need to both plan for and assess how well bilingual children are progressing. In order to do this they will need to carefully observe the children, taking notes of what is seen and heard. They should be alert to children using multimodality and translanguaging and take seriously what the children create or do or say as examples of children using what they know and can do in order to express and share meaning. Observing children means looking, listening and, essentially, recording in some way in order to gather evidence of what you have seen and heard. Observation notes need to be read through and thought about and analysed to decide the significance of what the child has said or done. Samples/examples/photographs can be used as part of records of what the child has achieved over time. Good educators will build a profile for each child to track progress over time. Such a profile will help notice what is going well and what might need more attention.

In other words practitioners should observe and assess bilingual children just as they do monolingual children.

In terms of multimodality, try to work out what the child is trying to achieve when she adopts different voices, dresses up, plays roles and tries out what it might be like to be someone else. It is important to ensure that many opportunities are made available for the children to engage in role play and story making.

Children can be models for one another so it is a good idea to consider how and when to set up peer teaching sessions where children can teach one another. To do this successfully you will need to identify what it is that individual children can do that others might like to learn to do. So look out for children who know something about their languages – written or spoken – and get them to take turns teaching this to one another. Or think of things individual children can show others about their culture – something like tell a traditional tale, sing a song, bring in an object, play a game or eat some home-cooked cakes/sweets/ treats. You might like to set up a system of peer mentoring where you ask a child who speaks the same language as a new arrival and is more fluent in English to become a special friend or mentor to a new arrival.

If you have any influence in the decisions made within the school or setting keep reminding people of the essential role that bilingual teachers or teaching assistants can play.

Chapter 10

The threat of a good example

Celebrating and supporting young bilingual learners

In his book *What Uncle Sam Really Wants* (1998) Noam Chomsky wrote a piece called 'The Threat of a Good Example'. It is a phrase that grabs your attention and makes you work hard to understand its implication. The good example is what I am hoping to offer you in this chapter and the threat is that it might seem impossible to achieve.

You may remember that the Bullock Report told us that schools should adopt a positive attitude to their pupils' bilingualism and wherever possible help maintain and deepen their knowledge of their mother tongues. It goes on to say that the school or setting that really welcomes its immigrant parents must also be prepared to welcome their languages, to display notices and other materials written in these languages, and even to adopt some of the rhymes, songs, games and stories learned by the young children at home. Let us go further than that and state that we should recognise and support all that bilingual children bring with them that will enhance their learning and that of their fellow students. Good education is essentially *dialogic*, which means that it involves more than one person in some exchange of information or ideas.

Jim Cummins, reporting on a conference in Komotini, Greece, in 1999, wrote this:

> The devastating earthquakes that had struck both Turkey and Greece in the weeks prior to the conference, and the mutual assistance given by each country to the other, perhaps had contributed to shaking up old ways of thinking. Expansion of imaginative horizons could perhaps also be read into the rapt attention paid to accounts from both the United States and Israel of similarly conflictual and oppressive social relations, and the possibility that educators could transform these coercive social relations into collaborative ones.
>
> (2000: 10)

Can you guess what aspect of these two examples, one in the United States and one in Israel, caused them to constitute what Noam Chomsky (1987) called 'the threat of a good example'?

> When schools and individual educators refuse to play their preordained part in the social order, education becomes dangerous. The discourses of national and religious identity, and the historical myths that sustain them, risk implosion when contact and dialogue replace isolation and monologue. When two languages are used in the school to affirm the experiences and cultures of the students and communities who speak those languages, this in itself challenges the discourse of superiority and devaluation that characterizes social relations between these communities in the wider society. To create a future we need to rupture the past.
>
> (Cummins, 2000: 10)

It is a poetic phrase but let us consider a recent event and think about whether we need to rupture the past or accept it for what it is but challenge it with other images. One night a student at Cape Town University covered an old bronze statue of a white man in excrement. The statue was, of course, of Cecil Rhodes – British diamond magnate, politician and unapologetic colonialist. A man who dreamed of a British empire, stretching from Cape Town to Cairo. You will have seen many similar defacings of depictions of events and people. The incident has caused a nationwide dispute about the legacy of apartheid. There have been critics and defenders, all passionate and all with some acceptable justifications. Albie Sachs, long-time fighter against the horrors of apartheid, listened carefully – as he always does – but then suggested that perhaps a more powerful way might be to keep the statue in place but surround it with other images that represent what has happened in South Africa since the apartheid regime was dismantled.

Coming from that culture, which was called 'separate development' (which is what apartheid means), I initially celebrated the removal of a statue reminding students of the iniquities of the past. But on reflection I think we are products of the past and if we are to really respect and celebrate bilingual learners we have to criticise the past and offer an alternative and better today. A good example is that Muslim children in Thrace have been receiving a bilingual education for the past 70 years. The threat in this might have been that the people of Thrace resented having to respect and celebrate a different language and culture. This did not happen. Possibly because the language of instruction is only a surface structure. Cummins (2000) tells us that coercive power relations – where one more powerful group has the power to force another group to do something – can be expressed just as effectively through two languages as through one. He asserts that real change will only come about when practitioners have themselves undergone some dramatic change in terms of how to work towards transforming the future lives and societies of their pupils. To illustrate the significance of this, Cummins (2000) offers the example of a young man who was teaching in a Pomak village, having come from another part of the country where he did not have experience of hostility between Christians and Muslims in the region. He found it difficult to interact with the students and felt that teaching from the set curriculum was achieving nothing for either the teacher or the learners. To try to remedy this he asked his students to teach him some of their language. Wanting to move away from coercive power he determined to establish a more dialogic relationship with his pupils.

Earlier in this book we explored the idea of bilingual children being offered or finding a 'third' or 'safe space' in which to use their languages. This concept, originally described by Bhabha (1994), is based on the idea that culture is always fluid and changing, constructed *dialogically* (between people) and *syncretic* (combining threads of experience) in the sense that it offers the possibility of bringing together sometimes opposing views. For our purposes we might see the third space as being where different languages and cultures come together, possibly clash, but have the chance to come to some resolution. The third space has been used in an attempt to understand, for example, what happens when popular cultural texts are incorporated into the school curriculum. Historically this third space was defined as a virtual location in which colonial authority (that of the more powerful) is challenged and hybrid identities are created. Such identities are made up of two or more elements. So this space is not a cohesive one but one of tension, competing powers and insurmountable differences.

One analysis of the concept of third space has been used to explore how the diverse worlds of home/nursery/school can be brought together in educational settings, with home being one space, school/setting being a second and the classroom in which home and school cultures meet being a third space. This seems much too crude for me because if it were so there is nothing to explain what brings about change – or hybrid identities. If that were true all classrooms would be sites of educational change. And, sadly, they aren't. Something has to happen in the third space – the classroom – for change to take place.

Here is an example, taken from the work of Guttiérez *et al.* (1999), which illustrates well the roles of conflict, the importance of an expectation of mutual respect and the horrors of name calling.

> One particular morning, conflict, triggered by a student calling another student a 'homo,' challenged a principal rule of this community of practice, the expectation of mutual respect. In the course of addressing this conflict, a series of student questions about homosexuality and human reproduction erupted. Ms Rivera (class teacher) recalls:
>
> … Some children started calling others names. So we engaged in a conversation about why people use insults. And after discussing the reasons – it's to hurt people's

feelings, and to make others feel bad, and to make yourself feel bigger than them, in whatever respect that may be – I told the children that in order for us to have the knowledge of what everybody knew, we were going to say, all of us, the worst word we knew to insult another person. And I started, to kill that anxiety of 'This is my teacher I don't …'. And so one of the children said 'homo' again. And immediately another child said, 'What is that?' And another child answered, 'It's when a man loves another man instead of a woman.' And something sparked so that before I knew it they were talking about how a baby is made and how the sperm needs to reach the egg. So at that moment I realised I needed to do something, because the first thing in my mind was, 'District! Parents!' and so the most important thing in my mind was, 'How do I stop this conversation without stripping them of that power of that incredible spontaneity of this interest? […] Before stopping the conversation I said, 'You know what guys, I want you to know, I want you to understand, how comfortable you just made me feel, because you have proven to me that we are friends. But I want you to realise that what we are talking about right now is something that society at large, parents, that parents are not comfortable with, and in order for us to do this we need to have permission from your parents.' And so I asked them, 'Do you really want to do this?' and they said, 'Yes.' *(A. Rivera, personal communication to the researchers, February, 1995).*

(Guttiérez et al., 1999: 291–292)

For me this is an excellent illustration of a good example being a threat to the existing order. The young people clearly had a need to clarify some of their confusion about love, sex and gender after one student called another 'homo'. The teacher had built an ethos of respect in the class and allowed time for a discussion about the issues that were troubling the young people, who were then invited to find the worst word they could and use it. The discussion then turned to their need to talk about how babies are made. And it was here that the setting up of this third space (for me a good example) was hijacked because of fear of what the parents would say about such a discussion in the classroom. I am sure I don't need to tell you that this is a classroom in the USA. There is an argument for the importance of the third space as a site for introducing children to the discourse of power, rather than seeing it merely as a metaphor for a space in which new, hybrid and challenging discourses are created. The third space could be better seen as a place in which academic points could possibly be challenged and re-shaped, but also give rise to the reconstitution of the everyday, out-of-school knowledge of learners. Places where children learn need to be thought of as places where, through looking, raising questions not necessarily verbally, making changes, exploring and talking, agreements are reached (again not necessarily verbally) and some change takes place. Do you remember the story of Gabriela, earlier in this book, who took hold of the possibilities open to her when the teacher selected a theme that related to her own home experience and allowed her to show how expert she was about her own life? Brooker (2003) writes that safe spaces are where the life experiences of bilingual children can be recognised and valued. The implication of this for practitioners is that the learning of the children at home, in their communities, in the languages they use, need to be recognised and respected. The strategies practitioners use to teach these children need to complement what the children bring rather than ignore it.

Parents of bilingual children are often choosing to try to retain as much as possible of their languages and cultures by sending their children to community schools out of normal school hours. These are called complementary, mother-tongue, supplementary or Saturday schools in the UK or sometimes heritage language or community-based schools. These schools often depend on teachers working on a voluntary basis in mixed-age, mixed-level classes with limited resources. For many children they are key sites of learning, but are rarely recognised or linked to mainstream provision. This means that they are likely to need support from families and communities, and community educators. They are places where bilingual children can find the third or safe space in which to demonstrate their linguistic flexibility.

There is some recent research which shows that teachers in complementary schools have a better understanding of how children's linguistic, cultural and real lives can be integrated into what they are learning when a more *holistic approach* to pedagogy is adopted. For example, Maylor *et al.* (2010) showed that teachers who build strong relationships with children and their parents and respond to their needs help them build strong identities as learners. Anderson *et al.* (2008) described the work of some complementary teachers who took a humanistic perspective to learning by designing their own curricula which, with a focus on multimodality, included the arts. This shifted the focus from written and spoken languages to the hundred languages talked about by Malaguzzi. Hall *et al.* (2002) found that complementary schools in Norway had high parental and community involvement and were regarded as very successful. Mainstream and complementary schools are beginning to build links in the UK (Sneddon, 2010) and there is much to suggest that complementary teachers could become partners with mainstream teachers to co-design curricula, since they bring a wealth of knowledge on how children's language, culture and identity can be used positively in learning, together with establishing strong links with parents and communities.

It is evident that all people live in several worlds at the same time, being part of different communities and operating with different languages, identities and voices. Kenner (2004a) talks of these as being *simultaneous worlds* and it is the bringing together of these worlds in the safe space that enables bilingual children to become fully participant members of the class or setting. There the child's language and culture, experience and relationships are all accepted and shared.

The term *syncretic curriculum* refers to the activities that can bring together the threads of the lives of participants to weave a new cloth. All children, regardless of country of origin, home languages, religion or life history, will have had some experience of what is being explored to be able to fully participate.

In many early years settings it is common to set up play areas where children can adopt roles and play out everyday events in order to make sense of them. You will be familiar with a home corner, for example. But the question arises 'Whose home is reflected?' Do all families eat whilst sitting round a table and using knives and forks? Remembering the importance of young children being able to build on their prior experience it is important to ensure that the play areas offered don't exclude some of the children. This is a transcript of what a group of students submitted after a group discussion about play areas or themes they had set up and that had proved successful or unsuccessful with bilingual children. This is the list one student offered me showing what her group had said about this.

- We always do Christmas with all the frills and this bothers me because at least half the children are not Christian.
- A Travel Agency: lots of the children had never been in one and some had never been on holiday.
- We had a theme on bread and that was great because everyone eats some kind of bread and we got parents in to bake their favourite breads and took the children to the local bakery.
- One term a student set up a garden centre. It was a nice idea but a lot of the bilingual children had never been to one and when the student noticed that some children were never using it she turned it into a garden, which was much more successful.
- We have a large group of Turkish children and one of the parents asked if she could bring in things from home to put in the home corner. She brought a special coffee pot, and little cups: Turkish newspapers; came in to let us all taste Turkish bread; covered the dolls beds with traditional Turkish blankets and lent us some Turkish picture books. After that a Bangladeshi mother offered to do the same the following term.

(Personal workshop notes)

The implications for practitioners

Since this chapter is about how best to support bilingual children it contains some suggestions for those of you working with young children.

1 In order for bilingual children to become equal members of their class culture it is essential that **parents, grandparents, siblings, carers and other family**

member are enabled to be supportive. They will also be adjusting to living in a new culture and possibly learning and using new language. Do approach them with respect, communicate with them appropriately, offer them a range of times to come in to watch what is going on, or talk to you, to ensure that they have a voice. It is difficult, of course, but resources are available to help with *translation* by asking older siblings or other community members to help. To create a culture of respect in your class or setting you need to do your best to **make parents feel that your class, your setting, is theirs too.** If possible make serious efforts to contact and reach parents and carers even though this might involve you thinking about how to present information to speakers of languages other than English and how to do this in a non-patronising way. You may need to seek professional help in terms of ensuring that translations are accurate. When inviting parents to come into your setting you might have to think about times of day that would suit them and ways in which reluctant women, in particular, might be supported in coming. My grandmother, newly arrived in a dead-end town in South Africa after leaving Russia, never went to anything at my mother's school. My mother, now aged 93, has still not forgiven her!

2   It is important too to be **willing and patient about talking to parents as best you can about how important the school thinks it is for children to keep using their mother tongue.** Be sure to tell parents that there is much evidence that this is the best way to ensure that your child will do well at school and learn English. Parents and people in the local community are a potential resource in terms of what they know about the children's home lives and experiences, their languages, celebrations, customs and beliefs. You may find them eager and willing to come in and help out by listening to the children read, play alongside them, become involved in activities round cooking or planting or making things.

3   Do take the trouble to **make contact with any complementary schools in your vicinity.** Visit them, if you can, to get an idea of which, if any of your children, might benefit from them. Talk, as a staff group, about the possibilities of finding speakers of the languages of your school or setting, who might want to come in to help, and talk to the management team to explore the possibility of employing them as primary helpers or classroom assistants. If possible try to get support to start an English language support group for parents in the school or setting or even just offer a space where parents/mothers can meet together to chat or play with their younger children or share issues. Try also to involve parents in the making of dual text books, writing books in their home languages, reading with children and more.

4   There are enormous difficulties associated with all of this and it is not possible to offer bilingual education to all pupils. But it is possible and

desirable to **teach primarily in English, encourage the children to use their mother tongues whenever they want to and provide support through employing bilingual teaching assistants or involving parents to help.** I am well aware that much of what has been said does not reflect the everyday possibilities of what teachers and practitioners can do in the real world and the purpose of including what 'best practice' might be is merely to offer ideas and thoughts. In some schools and settings in the UK and many other countries there are certainly more than two or three languages: there are often nearly a hundred. It is not possible for any class or setting to deal with these in anything other than a superficial way. But by forging strong links with the communities your school or setting serves, you will be better able to develop what would be regarded as good practice.

5   You can certainly **ensure that the resources you offer do reflect the cultures and languages of the children in your group**. There are many dual text books, books about life in other places, heritage language tales and songs. You can set up areas of the room to reflect the characteristics of the third space that will allow children to draw on their own experience. You can ensure that in your dressing up box or the clothes on offer there are things that will be familiar, open-ended so that they can be used to become anything – perhaps a length of cloth, a string of beads, a battered stick, a fancy hat. If you have a place where children can make music you can find or make cheap instruments – shakers, things to beat, things to blow, even things to pluck. If you play music in the room try to reflect music from all around the world. It is easy to find examples online.

6   Enrich your curriculum and the children's lives by **offering them opportunities to use their creative languages – to dance, move, draw, paint, make things, act things out, create visual narratives.** And do remember to always encourage children's use of their mother tongue. If you can afford it there are wonderful things to be learned from inviting a storyteller or a singer. Take the children to the theatre. Art galleries and museums are free. An outing to the local park or someone's garden offers much to explore – to look at, touch, draw or paint. Do remember that there are languages that are not dependent on words.

7   Remember that there are many studies showing that mother-tongue instruction – which means actual teaching in the child's first language – can improve a child's self-esteem and chances of doing well academically. There is evidence, too, that the fostering of L1 is important to overall language and cognitive development. Cummins (2000) showed us that mother tongue is fragile and easily lost in the early years of school. If use of mother tongue is discouraged children lose competency in that language. There is evidence too to show that where young children are encouraged to use their first languages in nursery and Key Stage 1 classes, in creches and with childminders,

they will start to explore literacy in the host language. **Talk to parents about encouraging their children to start reading and writing in their first language because we know that if they develop the early skills of reading and writing in that mother tongue the skills will transfer to their second language.** So a child becoming an early reader or writer in Urdu, for example, will transfer the skills to later becoming a reader or writer in English. UNESCO recommends that children should not be required to learn in a language other than their first language before the age of 6–8 years. Cummins (2000) said that children could be better introduced to a second language through it becoming a subject on the curriculum rather than the medium of instruction.

8　The **benefits of having an adult speaker of the language or languages in the setting or school are apparent and well-documented and cannot be overstated.** There are relatively few bilingual early years practitioners in our schools and settings. Conteh tells us that often these teachers are regarded pejoratively as being 'merely teaching assistants' and the vital contribution they bring with their metalinguistic knowledge and understanding is ignored. The advantages of having bilingual teaching assistants in schools and settings are now being recognised and more and more settings try to employ them.

9　And finally, but crucially, much **thought needs to be given to the future training of early years teachers and practitioners.** This should include a much greater focus on the importance of being able to both support and respect young bilingual learners. They need to learn more about languages, language acquisition, how best to support bilingual learners, and how to work with parents and carers. One thing is certain: our country is going to continue to be enriched by welcoming the languages and cultures of newcomers.

Section IV

Moving from the personal to the public

'We learnt the music of our language on top of the content'

(Ngugi wa Thiong'o, 1986)

In this, the last section of the book, we look at some wider political and philosophical issues that relate to much of what we have looked at on the level of the personal/individual, the home and community and the school or setting. We also look more analytically at some of the issues raised in the language histories in the first section of the book.

We start, in Chapter 11, by thinking about *children's rights* – not only language rights but also the impact of traditional Western views on child development and how these have coloured the ways in which we depict and think about childhood and adulthood, work and play, dependence and autonomy. This leads to a consideration of what can be done to help adults – parents and practitioners in particular – think more about children and their development globally, paying attention to often ignored issues like the effects of poverty, discrimination, ignorance, globalisation, emigration and being othered.

Following on from this, in Chapter 12, we revisit *the third space*, which you will remember is where the adult finds a way of inviting the child to reveal and celebrate her expertise in her own language and culture. We examine some research carried out in Berlin, on how young children 'perform' for an audience as a way of seeking to more clearly understand who they are. The title of the piece is *Performing Alienation: Performing Turkishness*. You are invited to read not only an account of the research but also how it was analysed. Do think carefully about what you can learn from this kind of deep analysis.

In Chapter 13 we take another look at the close links between *language and identity* to build on the example of young children performing alienation in the previous piece. We touched on language and identity earlier in the book but here we extend the concept of identity to include *national identity*.

In Chapter 14 we look at ways in which *language and culture can be preserved* in classrooms and settings, as well as in homes. We have already looked at what educationalists, practitioners and teachers can do. Here we consider the wider implications for policy makers.

The final chapter (Chapter 15) examines links between *poverty and bilingualism, poverty and exclusion, and poverty and pedagogy.*

Chapter 11

Which children? Whose rights?

The field of child development is something you may have studied as part of becoming an early years practitioner or as an interested parent or as an ordinary citizen. You will almost certainly have come across journalists and others writing, often in a very academic and possibly inaccessible voice, about how children learn and develop and you may even have attended a course on 'parenting', perhaps, or on 'the importance of play'. It is particularly important to be able to deal with this domain critically, because almost all of what you read in this area will refer to one set of norms and ideals – that of the developed world – and barely touch on what relates to the rest of the world. The underpinning image of this area of study for me is the image of the single child – Piaget's tireless little explorer – trying to make sense of the world that 'he' inhabits, moving from one stage of development to another. (I use 'he' rather than 'she' advisedly here.) Piaget's view has been very influential throughout the developed world and yet it pays scant attention, if any, to the social and cultural aspects of development. Although the roles of others in learning and development are mentioned, they are not deeply analysed as they are in the work of Lev Vygotsky and then Jerome Bruner and Barbara Rogoff, and still more recently Colwyn Trevarthen, all of whom remind us of the importance of interactions between learners and others, the impact of where the learning takes place and the underpinning values of any learning situation – in short, of culture, context and diversity. Nowadays we recognise that traditional views of child development do not offer us a blueprint for all children. We now know that we cannot identify *universal features* of either growth or change. Children will grow and change according to a wide range of circumstances – the food they eat, the climate in which they live, the work their parents do, the ways in which adults communicate with them, the beliefs and customs of their communities and their particular styles of behaviour and interaction. Theorists are now attempting to consider the realities of the lives of young children – for our purposes, young bilingual children – in both the developed and developing worlds, boys and girls, all trying to make sense of their worlds. One of the questions we need to ask is what rights young children do and should have. Too often those who have written about children's rights have made huge cultural assumptions about all children, often questioning the validity of any experience other than Western experience. All experience is significant and allows the child opportunities for asking questions, seeking answers and communicating with others. Much of the published research on child development comes from economically rich Western societies and it is important to remember that their view of what young children have experienced is based almost solely on an individualistic model of childhood, adulthood, autonomy, the role of parents and more. Child development theorists often examine the child moving from dependence to autonomy, which is seen as an important goal. Yet in much of the developing world young children achieve some degree of independence much sooner than children in the developed world. They often play adult-like roles in their society, contributing to the demands of daily life. Child development research has often taken place in laboratories, examining issues like the role of mothers, who are, in almost all cases, middle-class mothers, and who are depicted as engaging in one-to-one interactions with young children. In the developing world personal interactions like this occur, but are not seen as being more significant than other interactions. Western child development theories cannot be regarded as universal as accounts of mother/child interactions, parenting, play, work or family structures. Many children in the developing world are reared by grandmothers, siblings, neighbours, aunts and uncles. Some very young children have become the head of their household when parents have been killed in wars or died through contracting illnesses like malaria, Ebola or Aids. Some young children have been forced into becoming child soldiers or prostitutes. In the developed world much emphasis is placed on the value of play in the early years, prompting huge sales of toys that claim to be 'educational'. Yet children play wherever they are, with whatever is at hand, and learn just as much as those playing with manufactured playthings.

Bame Nsamenang (2011) is a respected writer on African children and their learning and development and it is sad that his work is so rarely cited in academic texts in the West. In his work, which is very often collegiate in the sense that he works alongside fellow academics across the vast continent of Africa, he charts and analyses the life experiences of African children. He always reminds the reader that almost all of Africa (Ethiopia is the exception) was colonised at one time or another and the legacy of this is lasting and almost invariably negative. In many African countries the children of the poor and powerless grow up being made to feel inferior. Racism and prejudice were and still are endemic. In the book he co-edited he noted that, in general, African parents do not consciously raise their children in terms of thinking of stages of development. Rather they create what he calls '*participative spaces*' in their everyday lives where the child can be the agent of her own learning and development. She will learn from all that takes place in her daily life, using those around her as models. In this way she is an apprentice to a more expert member of her community. If you have read any of the writings of Rogoff or Vygotsky this will be familiar to you. In most African cultures there is a strong oral tradition, so young children engage in learning to use spoken language, sounds, rhythms, rhyme, movement, actions and song in making and telling stories to make sense of the realities, opportunities and events of their lives. (To know more about this read the wonderful account of an invented game called *xoxisa* in Chapter 14.) Children like Lindiwe (in that account) discover, adopt and adapt the objects and devices used within their cultures to express something about their feelings and ideas and turn these into narratives that can capture and hold the attention of an audience. It is like the everyday theatre of their lives. And it is not far removed from the role play encountered and described in the developed world.

Many African children are treated as fully participative members of their communities, often doing real jobs like fetching wood or water, helping with making meals, growing things, caring for the baby and more. They learn to use real tools, which would be regarded as unsafe in the developed world, and to take responsibility for real tasks rather than 'playful' tasks. They are almost certainly more independent than more privileged children and have learned things from their life experiences that their peers in the West have not yet learned. Many of them attend school on a part-time basis and some have no access to schooling at all. But these childhoods – common throughout the world – are neglected by text books.

Children do have rights and these are enshrined in law. In the West we see childhood as being work-free: we tell our children that play is their work. We tend to think of those children who need to work to earn money to stay alive as being subject to 'child labour' – a phrase that carries connotations of exploitation and possible harm. Yet the parents of these children in the developing world may regard work as an important part of children's socialisation into their communities, preparing them for their roles as adults in the community.

The 12 rights of children (with thanks to Woodhead, 2005)

Drawing on what has been set up in law in this country or more globally I have devised a set of children's rights of my own.

Children's right no. 1

Young children should have the right to develop in ways that are appropriate to their cultures and contexts. We need to look at them from their starting places and pay attention to the many stakeholders involved in their learning and development. They have the right to be regarded as being competent.

This relates to Article 12 of the UN Convention on the Rights of the Child (UNCRC, 1989), which sees the importance of talking about the *competent child* rather than the 'needy' child, since being competent is more consistent with having participatory rights:

> States parties shall assure to the child who is capable of forming his or her own views the right to express those views freely in all matters affecting the child, the views of the child being given due weight in accordance with the age and maturity of the child.
>
> (UNCRC, 1989: Article 12)

Woodhead (2005) says that Article 12 offers one of the strongest challenges for those of us interested in or responsible for early childhood development. It is linked to Articles 13, 14, 15 and 16 on freedom of expression, thought, conscience and religion and the right to privacy and freedom of association, according to children's developing capacity. One implication of this is to remind us that even very young children have their own views on what is just, what is unjust; who has power and why; their own development and its relationship to the ways in which the adults in their world impose their ideas and views on them.

Childen's right no. 2

Young children have the right to be full participants in their own lives and respected for their individual and unique experiences. This means that they have the right to be heard – to speak for themselves, rather than be spoken for.

In recent years some researchers and writers have tried to include the voices of children in their work and attempted to have proper consultation with them but many of them end up being tokenist since they maintain the conventional power structures prevalent in Western societies and built around the agendas of adults. There are some significant pieces of research into the views of working children and the Open University's Children's Research Centre is worth looking at (http://childrens-research-centre.open.ac.uk).

Just to give you a taste of some of the work to be found on that website, this is how 9-year-old Kian Hamirani described the starting point for his small piece of research.

> I live in a gated housing society of several blocks of flats in a big city in India. My topic is street dogs. There are many stray dogs in India. Some of them live inside my housing society and others live outside on the street. I chose this topic because

they have their own life. They have their freedom.... Street dogs eating garbage don't need to have people throwing stones at them. The people should not kill them but keep them as a pet. Last time I saw a street dog who did not eat food for 3 days. I took him home and gave him half litre of milk and he drank it whole. He was licking the last few drops in the bowl and then I petted him for an hour. He is now my pet and has been inoculated.

(Hamirani, n.d.)

The UN Convention on the Rights of the Child (UNCRC) was drawn up in order to protect and promote the rights of all children across the world. It was the first international treaty to seriously consider the rights of children, recognising them as being able to participate fully in family, cultural and social aspects of life. It defines a child as a person younger than 18 years of age and applies to all children, whatever their race, religion or abilities; whatever they think or say, whatever type of family they come from.

Children's right no. 3

No child should be treated unfairly for any reason such as where they live, what language or languages they speak, what their parents do, whether they are boys or girls, what their culture is, whether they have a disability or whether they are rich or poor.

Children's right no. 4

When adults make decisions, they should think about how their decisions will affect children. This particularly applies to budget, policy and law makers. All adults should do what is best for children.

Children's right no. 5

Governments have a responsibility to take all available measures to make sure children's rights are respected, protected and fulfilled.

When countries ratify the Convention, they agree to review their laws relating to children. This involves assessing their social services, legal, health and educational systems, as well as levels of funding for these services. Governments are then obliged to take all necessary steps to ensure that the minimum standards set by the Convention in these areas are being met. They must help families protect children's rights and create an environment where they can grow and reach their potential. In some instances, this may involve changing existing laws or creating new ones.

Children's right no. 6

Governments should respect the rights and responsibilities of families to direct and guide their children so that, as they grow, they learn to use their rights properly.

Helping children to understand their rights does not mean pushing them to make choices with consequences that they are too young to handle. Article 5 (UNCRC, 1989) encourages parents to deal with rights issues *'in a manner consistent with the evolving capacities of the child'*. Governments are tasked with the responsibility to protect and assist families in fulfilling their essential role as nurturers of children.

Children's right no. 7

All children have the right to a legally registered name, officially recognised by the government. Children have the right to a nationality (i.e. to belong to a country).

Article 7 (UNCRC, 1989) states that children also have the right to know and, as far as possible, to be cared for by their parents.

Children's right no. 8

When adults make decisions that affect children, children have the right to say what they think should happen and have their opinions taken into account.

The Convention recognises that the level of a child's participation in decisions must be appropriate to the child's level of maturity. Children's ability to form and express their opinions develops with age and most adults will naturally give the views of teenagers greater weight than those of preschoolers, whether in family, legal or administrative decisions.

Children's right no. 9

All children have the right to a primary education, which should be free. Wealthy countries should help poorer countries achieve this right. Discipline in schools should respect children's dignity. Young people should be encouraged to reach the highest level of education of which they are capable.

The Convention says that for children to benefit from education, schools must be run in an orderly way – without the use of violence. It places a high value on education.

Children's right no. 10

Children's education should develop each child's personality, talents and abilities to the fullest. It should encourage children to respect others, human rights and their own and other cultures. It should also help them learn to live peacefully, protect the environment and respect other people. Children have a particular responsibility to respect the rights and cultures of their parents.

Children's right no. 11

Children from minority or indigenous groups have the right to learn about and practise their own culture, language and religion. The right to practise one's own culture, language and religion applies to everyone.

The Convention highlights this right in instances where the practices are not shared by the majority of people in the country.

What we learn from this

Governments should make the Convention known to adults and children. Adults should help children learn about their rights, too.

The role of UNESCO has been exemplary and they produce many reports and documents that are worth reading. They, too, emphasise the central role of mother tongue teaching and affirm that the maintenance of mother tongue is crucial to effective learning in schools and settings. They maintain a commitment to multilingual education and urge that the fundamental role of literary and academic proficiency in L1 will be the foundation for future academic success. In line with this they affirm the central role of parents as their children's first language teachers and urge practitioners to work with parents to help them become aware of the importance of maintaining mother tongue rather than allowing the child to lose the language in order to learn a second one. UNESCO also supports collaboration between minority language communities/organisations and schools and settings.

Chapter 12

Performing culture

Carmen Hogue, a friend of Marisa, said:

> My first language was Italian till age 6, then English, then Spanish from age 7 till 10 (when I lived in Mexico then Chile), then studied Tagalog living in the Philippines for nearly 3 years but kept up my English since age 7. I studied Spanish, French and Russian at University.

By my reckoning she learned six languages. She adds:

> I did not learn English in Italy when I was little because I was embarrassed when my parents spoke it, so they spoke to me in Italian. I forgot my Italian when I learnt Spanish but still understand some. I know a family, where the mother is Filipina, the father North American. They live in Mexico with two children who grew up there. The son speaks his mother's tongue fluently (Tagalog) because he identifies with her culture and sees Filipino food as his comfort food (even though they only visited the Philippines). The daughter speaks no Tagalog and has no real interest. She is very Mexican.

The world is full of remarkable people with stories like that of Carmen. She talks of having learned and lost languages and cites the example of a family where one of the children fell in love with the culture and language of the mother, while the other child remained immune to it. The push and pull of language and culture is very complicated. Young children, making sense of who and where they are in the contexts of their everyday lives, experiment with how the languages they use impact on those engaged with them.

Cleo Ganz sent me several additions to her original language history as she thought more and more about it. I was fascinated by how many issues were raised simply by answering the original questions I had asked.

> The more I think about how language had an impact on my life the more I realise how intricate the topic is. As I mentioned I grew up an atheist in a Jewish and half

Catholic family. My mother is Jewish and my father naturally Catholic, both not practising. Part of feeling special as a child in Italy was that my mother's part of the family was literally scattered all over the world and we always were in touch with most of these very interesting English speaking people. I eventually realised, maybe around 10/12 why. I've felt Jewish ever since. I've no religious background, no knowledge of Jewish traditions but a very strong Jewish identification. My mother finds it weird. I think of all the family that fled Germany and their children I'm probably the only one who went back to living there. I like to think that a circle has been closed and that my family is an example of how integration and understanding are possible. I think it is very important that my kids know their background because as my grandfather used to say 'it's important to never forget so that it can't happen again' and as his generation has gone it's even more important.

An unusual and revealing piece of research was carried out by Fikriye Kurban and Joseph Tobin from the Department of Curriculum and Instruction at Arizona State University in Tempe, USA. It was carried out in a kindergarten in what is described as '*a changing and socially and culturally mixed Berlin neighbourhood*' (Kurban & Tobin, 2009: 24) with a group of 5-year-old girls. They were the subjects of the study and had been drawn from a class where about half of the children were from middle-class German families, and an almost equal number were children of immigrants, almost all of Turkish origin. There were 28 children in the mixed-age class, ranging in age from 3 to 5. There were three teachers in the class, all of whom were graduates and had taken part in workshops on anti-bias and multicultural curricula. A seemingly welcoming and supportive environment for all the children.

The walls were covered with pictures from all around the world, the dramatic play area was stocked with clothes from various cultures – including headscarves – and ethnic meals are served at lunch. Every day during morning opening the teachers lead the children in greeting each other in various languages. On the wall there is a large map of the European Union that, surprisingly, includes Turkey as a member country, which we take as a symbolic gesture of welcome to the Turkish families whose children attend the school.

(Kurban & Tobin, 2009: 25)

Do you think we are looking at a good example carrying a threat?

This small-scale piece of research is interesting for many reasons. From what you have read so far you have every reason to think that this is a model of good practice. Certainly the researchers thought that too until they filmed a morning session consisting of various activities, including art, free play and a trip to the park. The film included scenes of the two groups of girls (German and Turkish) interacting happily but also scenes of the Turkish girls apart and in some places speaking to one another in their mother tongue. Then a fight broke out about who owned a hair-clip, at which point one of the teachers came over and the language changed to German. The video ended with a clip of the girls sitting down together at lunch and saying a Muslim prayer.

The film was played back to the children and the Turkish speaking researcher, Fikriye, then recorded a discussion with the two girls, Ayla and Selda – both born in Germany – which went like this:

> Fikriye: Did you like the video?
> Ayla: Yes, I did. But I didn't like the fighting part.
> Fikriye: Why?
> Ayla: Because that hair clip was mine and she took it from me. She always does that.
> Fikriye: What were you doing during lunchtime?
> Ayla: We were doing Quran.
> Fikriye: Why were you doing Quran?
> Ayla and Selda: We were praying.
> Fikriye: Why were you praying?
> [They both shrug]
> Fikriye: Do you play with the German kids?
> Ayla: No, we don't like them.
> Fikriye: Why don't you like the German kids?
> Ayla: Once I asked Lelesa if I could play with her and she did not want me. So we don't want to play with them.
> Fikriye: What if they want to play with you?
> Ayla: We speak Turkish. We speak Turkish so they won't understand and they will go away...
> Fikriye: Do you go to Mosque?
> Ayla: Yes, I go to Mosque.
> Selda: I go to Mosque, too.
> Fikriye: What about the Germans?
> Ayla: No. They don't.
> Fikriye: Why?
> Selda: Because they are not Turkish ... Germans go to, there is this thing [tracing a cross with her finger on the table]. They go there.
> Fikriye: Have you been to Turkey?
> Ayla and Selda: Yes.
> Fikriye: Do you like it there?
> Ayla and Selda: Yes.
> Fikriye: Do you like to live in Turkey or in Germany?
> Selda: In Turkey.

Fikriye: Why?
Selda: Because we have a lot of friends there.
Fikriye: But you have friends here, too.
Ayla: Here, it's only us.
Fikriye: Do the German kids like you?
Selda: They like us.
Ayla: No they don't. They don't like our body (Vücudumuzu sevmiyorlar). You know I am fat.

(Kurban & Tobin, 2009: 26)

I have slightly abbreviated this transcript, which I invite you to read and consider whether you think that these two 5-year-old girls feel liked and accepted in this setting, which seemed initially so welcoming to them and their culture and language. Here is what the researchers thought:

> Here we seem to have clear expressions of the alienation of these children and of mutual animosity between the German and Turkish children in this preschool. But we would suggest that there is both more and less going on in this transcript than meets the eye. When faced with such a transcript of children's talk, we cannot take everything the children say at face value. We believe in the importance of giving young children, and particularly children of recent immigrants, a chance to express their feelings about their early childhood education settings. But if we want to understand these children's perspectives, giving them the opportunity to speak, while necessary, is not sufficient. We need to work to understand what they say to us and we need to be cautious, to avoid oversimplifying or misunderstanding what they tell us. We must meet them halfway to interpret the meaning of what they are saying.

(Kurban & Tobin, 2009: 26–27)

What the researchers did next was carry out an analysis of all they had recorded using some of the ideas of Mikhail Bakhtin (1990), the Russian literary theorist and philosopher of language, whose wide-ranging ideas have significantly influenced our thinking in cultural history, linguistics, literary theory and aesthetics. The language used is quite dense and academic but, with careful reading, should be comprehensible. A Bakhtinian analysis involves four features, as follows:

1   *All meaning is made and can only be understood according to the context in terms of where the phrase or statement was made: by whom* (in terms of age, gender, ethnicity, language, class and more) *and the wider, more global issues that influence the whole exchange.* In this case study we have two small Turkish girls in the context of a classroom in a bilingual kindergarten in Berlin. The wider factors

could be the growth of Islam in Europe, and possibly the unusual presence of Fikriye, who is a non-German speaking, Turkish woman.

2   *The world is only half ours, which implies that we use what we have heard and what we know and we are creative, as language users, so we use the voices and thoughts and views of others.* Teachers, parents, friends or foes might offer models in terms of styles and voices to be imitated in order to build a performance. We might ask if these little girls are just parroting what they have heard. Or are they endorsing some views? Are they play acting? Is this mere fun? Or is there some serious and deep exploration of vital issues?

3   *The content of psychic life is social and ideological.* Put more simply this means that when we come to try to decode, understand, interpret and analyse we need to identify the stresses and tensions underpinning the exchange. In this case study, these could be the anxiety these young children had about being filmed and interviewed; their uncertainty about what they thought they ought to do and say, and so on.

4   *The answerability and unavoidability of interpretation.* The researchers explain this phrase like this:

> In order to make sense of any statement – spoken, written or painted – we must read it. And to read is necessarily to read into, for meaning making is a process not just of decoding, but also of interpreting. Making meaning of children's utterances requires us to respond intuitively, imaginatively and generously to their words. . . . For Bakhtin (1990), every statement is directed to an audience and yearns for an answer. To answer means to listen carefully and then reply, as best we can, even when we fear we have not fully understood what was said to us and even when we know that our reply is inadequate.
>
> (based on Kurban & Tobin, 2009: 27–28)

You might find the phrase 'read into' difficult to understand in this context. I suggest it means not just accepting the surface version but digging deeper to find hidden and perhaps painful meanings.

Despite the academic language used, the ideas themselves are not so remote and may be useful in making sense of what we see and hear. You may well have come up with some ideas as to why these little girls said what they did on the video when there was much evidence that they were well integrated into their peer group. The researchers analysed this event in terms of performance – seeing the children's play as acting or adopting roles, trying out some possibilities, exploring being someone different from who you are. They also looked at both girls doing what they called '*performing alienation*' and '*performing Turkishness*'. The little girls make it sound as though they feel alienated by and from their peer group but the reality is that they join in with the other children and are accepted by them. It is possible and even likely that they have closer links with the other Turkish children precisely because they see one another out of the kindergarten. So they are trying out alienation. As to performing Turkishness, the researchers suggest that the little girls put on a special performance for Fikriye, who, you will remember is not German, but a Turkish professional woman, which is something rare in their world. Perhaps the girls are trying to show her how very Turkish they are. There is another possibility, which is that the children intuited that the researchers were looking for evidence of alienation and so performed this.

Children learn to perform culture just as they learn to perform gender. They experience, notice and imitate what the norms are within their cultures and then try them on, just as they put on the dressing up clothes to act out roles in their own made up scenarios. But there is a sting in this tale. Fikriye carried out some interviews with the parents of these girls and you may be amused or astounded at what was said.

> Fikriye: Was there anything surprising?
> Ayla's mother: Yes, I was shocked when I saw Ayla praying. We never do that at home. I don't know where she got that. I am confused.
> Fikriye: Are you upset because of it?
> Ayla's father: No, not at all. It is just, we don't do it at home and you wonder how much they learn from other places.
> Ayla's father: They speak so much Turkish. I wasn't expecting that. They don't speak that much Turkish at home. It's really interesting.
>
> (Kurban & Tobin, 2009: 29–30)

How interesting is that? The two little girls are not lying or being deceitful. Rather they may be trying to work out what being Turkish means at a deeper level. They must hear talk at home and in their community about 'the old days', about the good things that have been left behind, the bad things that happened to make them leave, what they miss. I can well remember my grandparents, immigrants in South Africa, after fleeing fascism in Eastern Europe, talking nostalgically about the forests, the wonderful cakes, the deep red beetroots and despairingly about all that had been lost. So perhaps these children are exploring the lost worlds of their families in order to understand quite who they are. The kindergarten offers them a third space in which to do this.

The implications of this are evident. Take seriously what children – however young – say and do and try to understand what it is they are making sense of. This applies to what they say and also to what they do. No child is '*just playing*'. Playing is how children do the serious work of trying to find out who they really are and how they fit into this bit of the world they are in now. To do this they draw on their previous knowledge and feelings, on what they have seen and heard in all contexts, what their memories are and how they think their bit of the world works. This is cognitive work of the highest order.

What we learn from this

You might ask why this piece is here, in a section on policy makers – those who decide what and how young children will be taught. I made the decision to place it here because it is a reminder to those involved in making policy to keep up to date on research and to read carefully and widely, ensuring that they don't lose sight of our global world in all its diversity. We know the power of language and languages and we also know how easy it is to see the world through white Western eyes. Two little girls remind us of their existence and their astounding ability to find ways of exploring and explaining their identities. And two sensitive researchers invite us to find a multilayered way of analysing what we read.

Chapter 13

Language and identity

In Chapter 3 we looked at how language defines children. We explore this again here but add to it the aspect of national or cultural identity.

Fatih Hasbudak was 5 years old when his family was deported to Turkey. Born in the UK he was British but his parents had been labelled as being 'overstayers' when they failed to renew their permission to remain in the UK. In an attempt to avoid deportation pending appeals, the family went into hiding. There Fatih and his sister Zeynep were taught by a dedicated teacher from their school, as the school and friends found ways to keep the family fed, educated and hidden – until the day that their father was lured out of hiding to pick up a parcel at the post office, arrested and, almost immediately, put on a plane to Istanbul. A few weeks later the whole family agreed to leave and came out of hiding. Many, many years later, through the wonders of the Internet I found Fatih again and he sent me his very short language history, which contains this brief and revealing passage:

> Perhaps one of the most interesting things about both the languages I speak is that I feel the need to use a language specific name for each language. I don't remember if we spoke about this earlier, but I legally adopted the name Flint many years ago which made my life a lot easier in social terms compared to the use of a Turkish name, Fatih, here in England. That approach also affected and preserved my bilingual and bicultural abilities in many other ways.

In her language history Toula Markos described the complicated feelings she has about identity. Taken, almost forcibly, from Greece to Australia at the age of 5, she only returned when she was 24. You get a clear sense of the pain of leaving, of having to adapt and take on a new identity.

> My grandparents all spoke Greek and lived in Neapolis (or 'New Town', 'Naples'), a coastal town on the very southern tip of mainland Greece. Both were born in different small villages in the hills behind Neapolis and moved after they married

and had children. My paternal grandmother and grandfather were both born in Eliniko. My maternal grandfather was born in a small village in hills behind Neapolis. My maternal grandmother was born in Paradisi, a small village in the hills behind Neapolis. Her name was Angeliki (which translates as Angel, Angela or Angelique) and she loved saying she was the 'angel from Paradise'. My mum was born in Neapolis, Dad was born in Eliniko and both speak Greek.

Dad emigrated to Australia in 1956 and brought Mum and the three kids out in 1957. I'm the oldest. I have two brothers. I was dragged to Australia when I was 5, speaking Greek. I learned English at school. Had to go to afternoon school to maintain Greek. Studied French and German in high school, until matriculation, but also studied a bit of Italian, Japanese and Indonesian at school. Went on to complete a degree in languages (double major in Greek, with minors in Italian and Spanish). I speak Greek with my mother. I speak English to practically everyone else.

When I returned to Greece for the first time, at the age of 24, I organised to get a copy of my birth certificate. This was the first time I realised that my baptismal name was 'Stamatiki' (with the stress on the final 'i'). I had been called 'Matoula' or 'Matina' as long as I could remember. The diminutives of those names are 'Toula' and 'Tina'. Whenever anyone was angry with me, especially my maternal grandfather, they would call out 'Ma-TIIIIIIIIII-na'. I loathe that name and if anyone calls me that I cringe and relapse into childhood. You cannot stress the 'ou' in 'Mat-ou-la' and get the same effect. Anyway, very early in school, I got rid of the prefix Ma- and just used 'Toula'. That's who I am! I have just celebrated my 63rd birthday.

A great deal has been written, over the years, about the impact of language and/or culture on identity. Much of the work in this area has looked at older children so I was very pleased to come across a small-scale study (carried out by Rich & Davis, 2007) of two 6-year-old bilingual boys from two different Arabic speaking North African countries who were in a Year 1 class in a city school in the UK. The school had a small percentage of bilingual pupils, as the children were mainly white and English speaking. The researchers called the children in the study Mohammed and Ahmed. When the study started Mohammed had been in the UK for one year. His parents were postgraduate students, planning to take him and his older sister and baby brother back home when they had completed their studies. Mohammed and his sister both went to an Arabic school at the weekends run by the Islamic Centre in the city.

Ahmed, by contrast, had two older brothers and one older sister, all of whom were at a secondary school in the city. Born in the UK he had only been abroad on three occasions with the family, when they went to their country of origin for fairly long periods of time. The visits were to see extended family but there were no plans to return to live in North Africa. He also attended an Arabic school at the weekends.

In the spirit of always being critical of what you read, do remember that this is a tiny study – an analysis of how only two children constructed identities – so read it out of interest but be wary of drawing universal conclusions.

Both boys were constructing identities – one for the world of home, family and community and the other for the world of school, peers, learning and rules. The researchers talked to the mothers of each of the boys and both told them that the boys seemed generally happy at school but were not making as much progress as the mothers thought they should have been making. Mohammed's mother was disappointed at how slow Mohammed's learning of English, his second language, was, for example. And like many parents they felt that the children had been placed in the incorrect groups – where there were some children with learning difficulties, for example. As an aside you might like to remember that the placing of bilingual children in special needs groups is still quite common. Their needs are, of course special, but they are certainly not children having difficulties in learning per se.

Alarmingly both mothers expressed concerns about how they, as parents, were perceived by the school. They expected the school staff to be the experts on education and the very notion that they – the parents – would be active partners in their children's learning was unfamiliar to them. The school had done little to help them understand just what it was they were expected to do.

The two little boys developed three main strategies to define who they were in school and at home.

- The first was to **try to be as like the other pupils as possible**. In doing this they were doing their best to conform, to be accepted, to have a voice and an identity and not to be seen as different. They must have worked out just what it was that made them acceptable, and this strategy certainly worked in the sense that the teachers and other pupils were positive about them. One of the markers of their adaptive behaviour was the adoption of English as their language of choice in school. Here is an extract of what Mohammed said about a fellow bilingual child, in a discussion with one of the researchers (*I* in the extract below):

  I: Do you speak to him in Arabic at all?
  M: No! He speaks to me.
  I: Would it be helpful if you spoke to him in Arabic?
  M: I don't want to.
  I: Why don't you want to speak to him in Arabic?
  M: Because – I don't want them to – to hear.

I: You don't want them to hear?

M: Yeah. Hear me talk to him in Arabic – all of them.

I: Children in your class?

M: Yeah.

I: How would it make you feel if they heard you talking in Arabic?

M: Not good at all.

(Rich & Davis, 2007: 42)

The school operated no ban on the use of mother tongue and saw bilingualism as an asset rather than a disadvantage, but the two boys had picked up the more subtle attitudes to languages other than English and themselves began to discriminate against speakers of other languages. They were seeking to belong to this new, out of home community.

• The researchers identified a second strategy used by both boys in terms defining identity – that of **operating differently at home from at school**. They developed the need to assume at least two different identities – one for home and one for school. Mohammed's mother was shocked when both Mohammed and his sister insisted on having the henna put on their hands for a family wedding party removed before returning to school. Mohammed also asked his mother not to speak Arabic to him in front of his school friends. He tried very hard to keep home and school separate. He refused to take a dual text book home and insisted on using English at home despite the fact that the family always spoke in Arabic. As his mother said, 'I speak Arabic and he answers me in English. No one else in the family does this. It's very strange.'

• The third strategy was to **attempt to make links between home persona and school persona.** Like many bilingual children, Mohammed had a real fear of being 'othered' or alienated by peers and a longing to belong and both boys feared being alienated because of the way members of their family were perceived. Ahmed's mother, for example, said that he had no problem with the school itself but he did have a problem with his mother coming into the school. Perhaps the way she spoke or dressed or presented herself was different from other mothers and this made Ahmed feel different – and inferior. Perhaps the situation of Ahmed was a little less complex than that of Mohammed. He simply began to use English more and more at home and told the researchers that he was both North African and British. He had clearly resolved the clash between the two bits of his life by developing two distinct identities in an effort to sort out just where he was placed within each. The researchers suggested that he was possibly developing an identity that was different in some ways from those of other members of his family and creating some distance between home and school.

When we talk about the importance of home/school/setting links we need to emphasise the importance of taking account of the issues facing many families whose language and culture are not that of the school. We need to think of ways of making it evident that everyone is welcome and important.

In analysing their findings Rich and Davis tell us something we have already looked at in this book – the fact that children's skill at performance can be very persuasive. The children performing alienation and Turkishness were skilled actors and it is very possible that all young children are in situations that demand this. It is important not to accept at face value that children are well integrated into classes and settings. You need real evidence of this. Being 'othered' is so difficult and frightening that children become skilled at playing roles to cover their fears. Those working with young children may need to become more aware of how, if children seek to draw boundaries of any sort between the worlds of the home and school, they do this. Mohammed and Ahmed were proactive in constructing different identities to protect themselves and this links to the work of Edwards and Alldred (2000), who wrote about the process of *individualisation*, which allows even very young children to become social actors, responsible for their own project of identity construction – in other words, making identities to suit different contexts.

Mellie Preston is a friend of Marisa and, like many of Marisa's friends, multilingual. In these extracts from her language history try to identify phrases that speak of language and national identity.

My maternal grandparents both spoke Spanish (coming from Velez Malaga and Andalusia in southern Spain). Same with their parents, my great grandparents and my great-great grandparents. My paternal grandparents both spoke Catalan and Spanish [Catalan is an ancient language spoken in the north east part of Spain in a province called Catalunya (Cataluña) in Andorra, south of France and some places in Italy].

My paternal grandfather came from a town called San Carlos de La Ràpita, as I do. It is the penultimate town in southern Catalunya. My grandmother came from a town not far from and behind the mountain from San Carlos de la Ràpita.

My parents spoke both Catalan and Spanish. My mother used to mix both languages and my brother and I would find it very funny and somewhat normal, so much so that when my daughter learned Spanish she would do the same and even now still gets a little confused.

I speak Catalan, Spanish, French, Italian and English. I can understand some German and Romanian. I have a good ear for languages and dialects. My first language was

Catalan, which was spoken everywhere apart from school and church, as we were not allowed and church was in Latin. Spanish was compulsory under Franco's dictatorship and was spoken at school and at formal places such as with lawyers, doctors etc.

Since I left Spain 40 years ago, the Catalan language has become more prominent. All Catalan people had to go back to school and relearn how to write and read Catalan correctly. As I had left already, I did not get the chance to learn it again. In saying that when I email or contact my family and friends, they prefer I continue to communicate in my not so polished Catalan. I did feel somehow a little ashamed as I could not be as fluent as I would like, but with the current technology's aid I have now mastered [it].

There is more to this wonderful language history. Did you notice the delightful story about two of the themes in this book – translanguage and imitation? And were you able to find the paragraph talking about language and nationality? Authoritarian regimes, like that of Franco's Spain, sometimes make one language the language of the country and deny speakers of other languages the right to be full members of their society. It was the case, too, in apartheid South Africa. It still applies in many countries in the world.

What we learn from this

Most importantly we learn just how closely language is associated with identity, self-esteem and a sense of dignity. This is powerfully illustrated by Primo Levi (1989) in his book *The Drowned and the Saved* (quoted here from my book, *The Developing Child in the 21st Century*, 2013b: 109–110).

Levi was a survivor of Auschwitz, living for long enough to write poignant, powerful and bitter accounts of what he experienced and witnessed in the camp. Living with him in the camp were those whose first languages were Yiddish, Italian, Greek, Hungarian, French and German. The language of the camps themselves became something else – something unique – tied to the place and the time. And although the language of each camp differed in some respects, all denied the inmates respect for their language or identity. A German Jewish philosopher, Klemperer labelled the camp language as the *Lingua Tertii Imperii* – the language of the Third Reich. Levi observed that where violence is inflicted on people, it is inflicted on language. And vice versa. For the Italians in the camps attacks on the some of their regional dialects did much to damage their self-esteem. In Auschwitz the word to eat was *fressen*, which is the word used almost exclusively to describe what animals do. In Ravensbruck, the only camp exclusively for women, two words were used to describe them: one was *schmutzstuck*, which means dirty, or garbage, and the other *schmuckstuck*, which means jewel. You may have heard the term *Muselmann*, which literally means Muslim, but was used to describe those worn-out ravaged prisoners close to death. The reasons for this are unclear although Levi suggests they could refer either to fatalism or to the head bandages which might have resembled 'a turban' (Levi, 1989: 77).

Levi pointed out that having a language of potential use within the camps, for example, German, was not a luxury but a life-saving necessity. He noted that those prisoners who did not understand German died within the first ten days after their arrival. The fact that they could not communicate meant that they could do nothing to ameliorate their conditions: they may almost certainly have perished in any case. This is complex stuff and requires careful reading and thought. What happened was that those in charge, those holding the power – the Nazi *kommandants* – did not denigrate their own language of German – that civilised, sophisticated and respected language of Schiller and Goethe – but used a bastardised version of it. This enabled them to retain an image of themselves as 'civilised'. In stark contrast the prisoners, deprived of their liberty, families, hair, names and language descended into an impossible invisibility and anonymity.

In *The Truce* Levi, looking at what happened when the camps were liberated, described the tragic story of a 3-year-old child, Hurbinek, who 'was a nobody, a child of death, a child of Auschwitz' (1979: 197). He was alone, paralysed from the waist down, unable to speak at all. The name had been given to him and his eyes were full of anger and anguish. A 15-year-old boy in the camp tended to Hurbinek, brought him food to eat, cleaned him and talked to him slowly and carefully in Hungarian. After a week of doing this the older boy told the others that Hurbinek could say a word: what the word was no one knew, nor did they know what language it was in, but it was apparent the child was attempting to communicate. Levi tells us that the child experimented with making sounds – desperate to be understood – and despite the fact that around him in that abominable place there were speakers of nearly all the languages of Europe, no one could understand him.

> Hurbinek, who was three years old and perhaps had been born in Auschwitz and had never seen a tree; Hurbinek, who fought like a man, to the last breath, to gain entry into the world of men, from which a bestial power had excluded him; Hurbinek, the nameless, whose tiny forearm – even his – bore the tattoo of Auschwitz; Hurbinek died in the first days of March 1945, free but not redeemed. Nothing remains of him: he bears witness through these words of mine.
>
> (Levi, 1979: 198)

Chapter 14

Preserving language and culture

Adrine Santos, who is another friend of Marisa, wrote this rather sad reflection:

> When I was young I used to resent that my father was so insistent with us, forcing us to only speak Spanish in our home. Back then I did not understand that he was doing it as a way of helping us preserve our first language/culture.
>
> He also made us read books in Spanish, watch Spanish movies; my sister and I would also be the family interpreters and translators all the time, even the interpreters and translators for our parents' friends. It was funny and we got quite good at it. My father had a passionate commitment to maintaining the Spanish language. In retrospect I really wish I had insisted more like my father did . . . with my son. Funny how it is only later in life that we gain more insight and appreciation for language/culture.

We have talked in this book about some obvious ways of preserving and sharing culture and language in classrooms and settings by displaying different scripts and alphabets, introducing materials from the cultures of the children, inviting in speakers of the languages of the group and more, but I want to turn now to something that amazed and entranced me when I came across a chapter called 'The Pen Talks My Story', written by Susan Harrop-Allin (2014), in a new book on multimodal approaches to teaching and learning.

Having been born and educated in South Africa, the country and its enormously rich range of languages and cultures still tug at my heart. As I have already said, I went back there in 1995 and spent 3 years working throughout the country, considering what essential qualifications all early years workers should have. The standards we drew up eventually became law and for me this was the best time of my professional life. I learned more there in 3 years than I did either before or after. Much of what I learned related to my own self-esteem. When I started working in South Africa I regarded myself as something of an expert on child development. It was only with experience and the wisdom of my boss (who sent me off with a real expert and a moderator to argue our respective cases) that I realised how narrow my Western education had been. And, consequently, how narrow my view was.

It was the title of the chapter that grabbed my attention. '"The Pen Talks My Story": South African Children's Multimodal Storytelling as Artistic Practice'. On first reading I quickly recognised that it was not looking at young children but rather those aged between 11 and 12 in an urban school in Soweto. The author, Susan Harrop-Allin, is a musicologist who was doing research into musical games in playgrounds and classrooms when she noticed that the desks in the school were punctured with little holes. When she enquired into this the teacher told her that the children played what she called 'story-games', using pen and paper to draw grids or blocks and then making the pen, with enormous energy, create marks, dots and lines as the story was created. The paper with the marks on becomes a record of the story that the child has invented and performed. The name given to these graphic stories is *xoxisa*. Harrop-Allin tells us that *xoxisa* is a map that is effectively carved into the desk and also '*a sophisticated sign system that produces a form of narration connected to the township context and, thus, to children's lives*' (2014: 20–21).

It seems to be part of a whole repertoire of music/dance games that children play, and although the children clearly create, agree on and use some formulae or rules, it can be seen more as a creative genre than a game. It is a sound story – an oral narrative – which uses visual, kinetic, sound and dramatic devices.

The chapter focuses on one child, Lindiwe, who, like her peers, lives in a largely oral culture where storytelling and story making are everyday events and where, in telling the story, the storyteller may draw on her own life, what she has seen and heard in her community or on television. She uses the language of the streets – in this case a language known as *scamtho*, which is a mixture of Zulu, Sotho and English and is regarded as a marker of urban or township identity. Harrop-Allin videoed some of the *xoxisa* performances and had some informal interviews with Lindiwe and her peers and was assisted in making sense of it all by speakers of the languages who could interpret and explain possible meanings. The use of a pen to effectively *talk the story*, using dots and lines on paper, is a convention created by the child storytellers. What the viewer sees is a page divided up into squares – effectively a grid outline – on which emerge events, characters, places and spaces. It is the movement of the pen and the marks it makes that transmit the significant elements of the story. These may include the developing plot, the characters, the dialogue and the affect. Sample grids show 'before and after' the performing of the story, which illustrate how a framework has become a whole event. The blank blocks of the 'before' grid are changed by how the pen has been used in the telling. Often the tales are about real events so that fights and bullying are represented in the fierce and penetrating stabbing marks made by the pen, or arguments tracked; issues resolved. Lindiwe is creating a multimodal text in that she is using different materials available to her and varying her actions so that something like the rhythmic intensity of the pen's movements enables her audience to interpret what is being done. She moves between different sign systems and creates links using movement, voice, gesture and mark making. We are used to seeing young children doing this as they make sense of their world. We may not pay enough attention to this, often seeing it as random. What could be more random than dots made on a desk? Yet when we analyse what we see, and do this taking account of who we are looking at and what we know about her and her culture, language and experience, we begin to get a clearer indication of just what it is the child is doing.

The telling of a story using what is at hand becomes an incredibly complex cognitive act. It tells us just what the storyteller understands about her world, her place in it, her ability to take control of it and manipulate it to her own ends. It allows her to draw on her own cultures without value judgements to reflect her thoughts about events and issues that interest or concern her. There is no right or wrong way: rather there are conventions developed by the storymakers, drawing on their cultures. The learner – the child – is at the heart of the process, entirely in control of what happens. Cope and Kalantzis (2000) tell us that if we want to understand and use this to help us change our pedagogical approach – or the ways in which we teach or support learning – we need to recognise and value what the child is doing and help her become the director of her own creation. Lindiwe, in her making, using her pen to tell the story, was in complete control of the whole episode. She was the director of her own theatre, the author of the play and in control of all decisions. Cope and Kalantzis (2000), who talk about *multiliteracies*, see the task of the educator to be that of examining *design as a process*.

What Lindiwe was involved in was the making and sharing of meaning. In doing this successfully she needed to consider the language she used, what her audience would see and hear, what movements to make, how to indicate and use space and what other effects could be introduced. She also had to consider who her audience was so that she could choose how to present her story according to what she thought her audience would most appreciate. In one sense she had to develop and use a set of rules or a *grammar for xoxisa*.

Cope and Kalantzis (2000) talk of four associated things that need to be considered when thinking about how we can teach, starting with what the child brings. They are what they call Situated Practice, Overt Instruction, Critical Framing and Transformed Practice:

*   *Situated Practice* is what the child says or does, makes or creates.
*   *Overt Instruction* is just what it says: scaffolding the child's learning to build on what the child can already do to allow her to take the next step. For the child it involves systematic, analytical and conscious understanding.

- *Critical Framing* is inviting the child to look at what she has done and see what pleases her or what makes her feel she could do more.
- *Transformed Practice* means what the child does next that shows her learning has moved on. It is a rather wordy way of describing what we might already think of as good practice.

Certainly good early practitioners draw heavily on what the child has done, said, made or attempted and, by engaging with the child about what she has done or made, this validates what the child has done and allows her to reflect on what to do next. We might call the case study in this chapter an example of '*multimodal meaning-making practices*', as Jewitt (2009: 20) does.

Much of what is written about multimodal thinking focuses on the meaning maker. I am very much interested in the meaning sharer and what this means: since making meaning very often involves another person to watch or listen, join in or add to.

Colwyn Trevarthen has written widely about how infants become expert communicators, attuned to the features of their social and cultural worlds from birth. He has written about the significance of the mother's voice, heard or sensed even before birth and, in a delightful piece written jointly with Maya Gratier, he goes on to examine how voices admit the child into her culture.

> The mother's voice is also the voice of her community. It carries the history of her affiliations. A voice is never one's own ... it carries the imprint of close others and communities of belonging through styles of speech, accent, the recurrent use of words or turns of phrases, etc.
>
> (Gratier & Trevarthen, 2007: 176)

We are thinking about not only voice but the sounds made by voice – the sounds of the child's first language or languages. From the first non-verbal dialogues the infant holds with significant others, Trevarthen and Gratier argue that a process of *belonging* is set in motion. As they explain it, '*As the infant interacts meaningfully with close others, culture begins to inhabit its body and voice*' (2007: 176). They state that the vocal dialogues of 2-month-old infants carry the imprint of the specific conversational styles of the cultures they were born in (Cowley, Moodley and Fiori-Cowley, 2004; Gratier, 2003). You may well have come across the ideas of Bourdieu (1977), who talked of *habitus*, which means the rules that govern social behaviour. With infants, the researchers are talking of *protohabitus*, which would be the first set of rules for social interaction and exchange that the infant can predict from earlier interactions. It would seem that *protohabitus* grows out of the innate need for sharing meaning and this inducts the infant into her community. In the case of a bilingual infant, one would suppose that the child is soon able to predict two distinct sets of rules according to each language/culture. Gratier and Trevarthen (2007) talk of the rhythms of parents' vocal styles, which they say, '*carry cultural meaning, like flowing rivers, though ever changing, have memories, carrying minerals and sediments from other places and other times*' (2007: 176).

What we learn from this

The words of Gratier and Trevarthen sum it all up:

> Belonging is first played out in the body and the voice and in the anticipations of how and when the bodies and voices of others will behave – how the game will be played and how the rules may change or endure. Culture is in the body and in time before it is reflected upon and talked about in consciousness, or literature. This is why culture runs deep and languages leave their traces in rhythmic feel and anticipatory emotion, in life and literary art.
>
> (2007: 176)

Chapter 15

Pedagogy, politics and poverty

This, the last chapter in the book, starts with the language history of Marisa Mottola, who, despite not knowing me, went to extraordinary lengths to pass my questions on to her many bilingual friends in Australia. Very economically it tells of many of the themes of this book and in it you will find reference to all three of the themes of this chapter – pedagogy, politics and poverty.

> My mother migrated from Spain to Argentina in the 1950s. She was born in Zamora in the region of Castilla. My mother only spoke Spanish. My maternal grandparents spoke only Spanish. My father was born in Argentina and he only spoke Spanish. My paternal grandfather was born in Salamanca in Spain and he only spoke Spanish. I think that my paternal grandmother was born in Argentina, but from Spanish heritage.

> I speak Spanish and English. I learned Spanish at home and school and learned English in Australia at the age of 23. I knew some basics of English (mainly writing) but not spoken English and certainly not Australian colloquial English.

> I learned to speak Spanish with a Spanish accent (from my parents) and also with an Argentine accent that I learned from my friends and thought that this was what everybody did. However, when I went to school I realised that having a Spanish speaking accent had a stigma as many more recent Spanish migrants were poor and migrated to Argentina for a better life after the civil war. In contrast the people who spoke Spanish with an American or English accent were respected.

I asked Marisa to tell me more about the effect of politics and poverty on her and her family and here is some of what she said:

> Public education in Argentina is highly regarded, and perceived by the working class as the bridge to a better life. It is free at primary, secondary and tertiary levels. Argentina has one of the lowest levels of illiteracy in Latin America. But I believe

that poverty has an impact on the way you are treated, and this includes the way you are treated at school. In Argentina class is discussed often, much more than in Australia. Historically Argentina followed the idea of European supremacy, believing the country was 'discovered' by Europeans, therefore did not exist before Cristobal Columbus arrived. Racial discrimination is very often related to poverty. Racism is widespread and it manifests in many ways, in particular in the way that people are defined with derogative terms in relation to their origin, a reflection of their economic status. For example, there are words that define migrants such as those coming from Spain 'Gallegos' (Galician), after the wars in Europe. Nowadays this term is not used as often for people with a Spanish accent, or it does not carry the same derogative connotation as before, as the economic situation of the Spanish people that come to Argentina now is different to the one that was experienced by earlier comers. The recent Spanish arrivals will be perceived as having money. Indigenous people and African descendants are also called different names.

In Australia, learning English was necessary for my survival. Australia was not my culture and there are so many things to learn at the same time, not just the language. The pressure to learn a language as quickly as you can was high and I am sure it did have an impact on the way I felt about life at that time. Working and adjusting to a new way of life was also important, so English was learned at the same time that all the mentioned stressors were taking place. I wonder how I did not lose my mind!

You asked me about poverty in my family history. My grandparents were all European and poverty was an issue. My maternal grandparents lived under Franco and my paternal grandparents migrated to Argentina from Spain (Salamanca). Most probably because of the same issues related to the civil war. My paternal grandparents were illiterate and taught themselves to read and write. My grandfather eventually opened the biggest bookshop in the city. I still wonder how he did it.

What I am certain is that Spanish Civil War had a profound impact on my mother's psyche and how she trusted and perceived the world. By no means were we wealthy, but we were never poor. That was something my mother never understood. She always bought essentials as if she was ready for the war. We always have an enormous amount of sugar, oil, soap, etc. ready to cover our needs for the next coming year. I feel that the way she spends money was very much determined by her war experience. I think that a war situation says a lot about the politics and the economic situation of the country, and this has a huge impact on your motivation to learn and the capacity to overcome the experience in order to move on and be able to undertake further studies. But also has to do with the options you have in the host country and how the environment around you supports you being included as a member of that society.

Politics and poverty run through this as where Marisa reflects back to her realisation that the way you speak can carry a stigma related to your personal history of poverty and war. In many of the language histories those looking back one or two generations discovered that something drove their grandparents or perhaps their parents to move from one country to another and it was either in search of freedom or access to work.

Poverty often played a huge role. In the case of both my grandfathers, either discrimination or a financial crisis launched them into the upheaval of moving countries. I know that both my father's father and my mother's father went first, in search of a job and a place to live. They each then sent for his wife and the seven or three children. Politics, too, played a role, because for both sides of the family extreme anti-semitism forced them to re-locate – and when the holocaust came they were the lucky ones to have escaped. As to pedagogy, my maternal grandfather had left school at a very young age – like Janos – but became an extremely well-educated, self-taught critical and thoughtful adult. He ensured that his oldest child was partly home schooled in Russian, some German and some Lettish before she fled the country, where she quickly learned English. This pattern of people fleeing their homes is being seen now on a global and terrifying scale.

As I write this, newspapers are giving us the most up to date statistics on child poverty in the UK. We know that many of the bilingual children in our schools and settings come here as their families seek a better life. They may be asylum seekers, refugees or economic migrants. And many of them are speakers of languages other than English. One in every two youngsters in the most socially deprived areas live in families struggling below the poverty line, according to research that maps the extent of financial hardship in the UK. There is evidence that a quarter of all children in the UK are living in poverty. In some inner city areas this figure may be as high as 50%. In June 2015 we were told that these child poverty figures have barely changed. It will not surprise you to learn that many of the areas where child poverty is very high are in the East End of London – a starting place for immigrants from generations back. Nine of the 16 most deprived neighbourhoods, all of which have child poverty rates over 50%, are in Tower Hamlets, where the wards of Bethnal Green South and Bromley-by-Bow record rates of 54%. The other areas of concentrated poverty are in Westminster, Oldham, Leeds, Middlesbrough, Burnley, Pendle, East Lindsey in Lincolnshire and Thanet in Kent.

Jim Cummins was invited to visit South Africa to examine how their policy of retaining 11 official languages was working. As one would expect, much of his work there focused on how those who had been, for generations, marginalised, excluded and isolated by the apartheid system are doing in the schools and settings of the 'new' South Africa. By definition all had – and to a large extent still have – low socioeconomic status, still live in poverty and still have inadequate access to healthcare and nutrition. They are largely still housed in particular areas and enduring a lack of what Cummins calls '*cultural and material resources in the home*' (2015b: 226). The government in South Africa set a goal of 100% primary school attendance by 2015 and recent figures show that they reached this target. The children in primary school largely come from poor homes, with limited access to print within both homes and schools/ settings. Their communities suffered long-term and extreme discrimination, but with the coming of the new government there has been a tremendous affirmation of the differing cultures, although not of differing languages to the same extent. One effect of this is that many of those now at universities, schools and settings do not fully accept the educational legitimacy and the academic relevance of their home languages. This is a deeply worrying effect. They are still hindered by sensing that the wider society does not regard their languages as fit for learning. If we extrapolate from these ideas to our schools and settings we find similarities in that many bilingual children and their parents and teachers feel that their home languages are inferior to those of the mainstream. It seems that poverty alone can negatively affect the educational opportunities available to young bilingual children.

But there are other factors at play. Immigrant communities still often have to deal with being marginalised by the host community. They may encounter racism, being jeered at, bullied and othered. Teachers and practitioners may have low expectations of the abilities of the children largely because they may not understand clearly that these young speakers of languages other than English are as intellectually able as English speaking children. All linguistic experience is equally valuable. There will be many children in our schools and settings who have lost or are losing their *indigenous languages*. Alfredo Basile is a friend of Dario Iacopucci and his detailed language history is included particularly for its mention of one of the thousands of lost or endangered languages. It is written in a very informal voice and I have retained that because it makes the reader feel closer to the writer.

Mmmhhhmmm, this is going to be a long reply because both my father's family and mother's family had ancestors who migrated from Italy to different countries. My maternal grand-grandfather used to travel and established a trading business in South America (Venezuela) and central America (Panama). He used to speak Italian and Spanish. He came from a rich family and he became much richer with his trading in those countries. His sons and daughters were all very well educated, but I'm not sure about him. My paternal grandfather had a brother who migrated to New York and he followed him. I don't know much about him because he died when my father was 3 years old, but I met my father's cousins who were born and lived in NY all their life and they told me that their father could not speak a good Italian, but only the Calabrian dialect. I think they spoke broken English.

My parents are both graduates and we have always spoken in Italian at home. My hometown is in the south of Italy where most people used to speak our regional dialect (Calabrian), but we had also a big Influence from the Albanian people who escaped from Albania in 1600 and came to our region. We still speak that ancient language which does not exist anymore in Albania. My father grew up as an orphan and he used to speak Calabrian with some of his friends and Arbëreshë (ancient Albanian) with some other friends, but at home we were allowed only to speak Italian.

I speak Italian, very bad Calabrian and Arbëreshë, Spanish and English. I learnt Spanish through an ex-girlfriend and also because I worked with some Spanish companies for few years. I learnt very poor English at school then I went to London for 6 months where I studied a bit and worked as a waiter. My English only improved a lot only when I started my current job in 2001. I have two children – one who is 2½ years old and already speaks two languages (very fluent Italian and good enough Russian), because my wife is Russian. The second one is 2 months old, so … not talking yet.

Like Lettish, Arbëreshë is a language I had never heard of before and that of an ethnic and linguistic Albanian minority community living in southern Italy, especially in the regions of Apulia, Basilicata, Molise, Calabria and Sicily. They are the descendants of the Albanian refugees who fled Albania between the fifteenth and eighteenth centuries as a result of the Ottoman empire's invasion of the Balkans. Immigrants fleeing from oppression, again. Today, experts suggest that there are probably fewer than 10,000 speakers of the language left. Does it matter if a language dies out? Many years ago I attended a conference at which Tove Skutnabb-Kangas was speaking. Born in Finland and raised as a bilingual Finnish/Swedish speaker she became very aware of the impact of the loss of a language to a culture, a country and individuals. She talked of *language genocide* – a term that horrified me at that time. But let us think about it more carefully. What happens when a language dies out because there are fewer and fewer speakers of the language? Is that a loss to individuals alone or is it more serious than that? Joshua Fishman, as long ago as 1994, talked of what happens when a culture loses its language. He asked if losing a language was like losing a handkerchief? A handkerchief can be replaced. But a language that has been long associated with culture is best '*able to express most easily, most exactly, most richly and with more appropriate overtones, the concerns, artifacts, values and interests of that culture*' (Fishman 1994: 72). You may remember how Mike Rosen, Anne Sassoon and I all talked of how Yiddish, a language that was said to be dying out, struggles to survive and is thought by all its users to uniquely capture some aspects of the culture – its jokes, its food, its tragic history. In some way the language itself comes to symbolise the culture. A language is also about kinship. My granny spoke Yiddish to me; my mother sang me Yiddish songs; my father told me Yiddish jokes and my parents would speak to one another in Yiddish when they didn't want me or my brother to understand what they were saying. This meant that we were both particularly interested to learn what they were saying and so we learned many Yiddish words and phrases as a means of feeling included. There is much about language that concerns belonging and sharing a sense of community – what some people call *gemeinschaft.*

In some cases the death of a language has been fiercely and sometimes successfully fought off. Maori, which is an indigenous language of New Zealand, has been saved through the work of educationalists who have fought over generations to ensure that its death can be denied by offering mother tongue (Maori) use in early years provision. Once a language has died out it is very difficult for it to be resuscitated. One example is what happened in Franco's Spain when Basque schools had to become underground schools since it was prohibited to use Basque in public precisely because the Basques had openly resisted the dictator. Speakers of Basque were shot in the streets; their language was outlawed and mocked but they resisted by setting up primary schools and preschools; healthcare provision, care for the elderly and more. They created an underground competitive system – their own cultural space.

What a lesson for us – one that Fishman puts in his own inimitable fashion: '*What are you going to do with the mother tongue before school, in school, out of school and after school so that it can be passed on from one generation to another?*' (Fishman, 1994: 81).

To end this book I return to politics. The profound ideas of Donaldo Macedo and his co-writer Lilia Bartolome (2014) deplore the fact that most multicultural educators have not undertaken any critical analysis of the politics of language and its role in education. They ascribe this to two factors: the teaching of *cultural tolerance* per se and the lack of political clarity in the bilingual education movement. This has meant that those making decisions about the education of bilingual learners do not understand just how neocolonial language policy has shaped and still is shaping bilingual language teaching globally. Neocolonial means the use of economic, political, cultural or other pressures to control or influence other countries, especially former dependencies.

Teaching tolerance is an interesting idea and it is not only paternalistic and patronising but it ignores the imbalances in power between the teacher and the taught. It implies an attitude of '*I will tolerate you even though your culture is repugnant*' (Macedo & Bartolome, 2014: 26). It fails to look at the huge economic differences between the developed and the developing worlds – the first and third worlds – aspects of which we see dramatically in the unpredictable immigration patterns that have exacerbated and still are exacerbating racism and xenophobia. Look at France, where the ultra National Front, headed by

Le Pen, is mounting continual attacks on immigrants, primarily Muslims from French colonies. The Turks, as I write, are bombing the Kurds. In Russia and Austria and some Scandinavian countries the level of anti-semitism is on the rise and the UK insists on turning its back on those fleeing suffering in their home countries in Africa or Asia only to risk almost certain death on leaky and overcrowded boats seeking refuge in wealthy, developed Europe.

Macedo and Bartolome examine the problems engendered by what they call 'scientific objectivity'. The phrase is in inverted commas to suggest just how this approach is neither scientific nor objective. It is a way in which educators, well-intentioned but naive, praise some superficial aspects of cultures while ignoring essential issues like class, culture, identity and equity. As Paolo Freire (1998) said, '*(they often) try to "hide" in what (they) regard as the neutrality of scientific pursuits, indifferent to how (their) findings are used, even uninterested in considering for whom or for what interests (they) are working*' (1998: xii). A friend of mine has a grandchild who has become reluctant to go to school and reluctant to read. Now aged 6, she was in love with books and stories and just starting to read when she went to school. She is privileged and monolingual. At school she was told not to read until she could 'do her phonics properly'. But now she is convinced that she can't read and doesn't ever pick up a book.

The phrase 'then I went to school' appears in the writing of many people whose experience of early education, particularly in former colonies, was one of suffering a fracturing of cultural identity. Being told not to use their first language in order to learn in the school language can be a trauma that is never overcome. My father used to tell us over and over about how, when he could not answer a question in English, the teacher pulled him up by his ear and said, in Afrikaans, 'Staan donkie' – which means 'Stand, donkey'! Although he overcame that he always found being in formal learning situations threatening. This fracturing of cultural identity often takes place when a child's experience, language, culture and background are disregarded or denigrated.

The examples that follow come from the work of Macedo and Bartolome (2014: 31–32). The African writer Semali said:

> Then, I went to school, a colonial school, and this harmony was broken. The language of my education was no longer the language of my culture. I first went to Iwa Primary school. Our language of education was not Kiswahili. My struggle began at a very early age constantly trying to find parallels in my culture with what was being taught in the classroom. In school we followed the British colonial syllabus. . . . Thus one of the most humiliating experiences was to be caught speaking Kichagga while still in the school grounds. The culprit was given corporal punishment – three to five strokes of the cane on the buttocks.
>
> (Semali & Kinchloe, 1999: xii–xiii)

Ngugi wa Thiong'o laments the loss of the language of Gikuyu in Africa:

> We therefore learnt to value words for their meaning and nuances. Language was not a mere string of words. It had a suggestive power well beyond the immediate and lexical meaning. Our appreciation of the suggestive magical power of language was reinforced by the games we played with words through riddles, proverbs, transpositions of syllables, or through nonsensical but musically arranged words. We learnt the music of our language on top of the content [...]
>
> And then I went to school, a colonial school, and this harmony was broken. The language of my education was no longer the language of my culture.
>
> (1986: 11)

What can we educationalists, parents, researchers, policy makers, writers and community members do, then, to ensure that future generations of bilingual children do not grow up thinking that going to school was the beginning of them losing their language, culture and identity? We need to recognise the damaging effects of colonialism, capitalism and globalisation and work towards a recognition of the richness of languages and cultures other than ours. We need to recognise and challenge the ever-growing dominance of the English language but also invite our young children to keep using their first languages and persuade their parents of the importance of this. Perhaps this means that cultural production, and not reproduction by imposing English, is the only means by which we can achieve an education system that is culturally democratic. A system really fit for all.

Bibliography

Anderson, J., Gregory, E. & Kenner, C. (2008) The National Languages Strategy in the UK: are minority languages still on the margins? In C. Helot & A.-M.de Mejia (eds), *Integrated perspectives towards bilingual education: Bridging the gap between prestigious bilingualism and the bilingualism of minorities* (pp.183–202). Bristol, UK: Multilingual Matters.

Archer, A. & Newfield, D. (eds) (2014) *Multimodal approaches to research and pedagogy: Recognition, resources and access.* New York and London: Routledge.

Baker, C. (2011) *Foundations of bilingual education and bilingualism* (5th edn). Bristol, UK: Multilingual Matters.

Bakhtin, M.M. (1990) *Art and answerability.* Edited by M. Holquist and V. Liapunov. Trans. Vadim Lyapunov and Kenneth Brostrom. Austin: University of Texas Press [written 1919–1924, published 1974–1979].

Ball, J. (2011) *Enhancing learning of children from diverse language backgrounds: Mother tongue-based bilingual or multilingual education in the early years.* Commissioned by UNESCO Education Sector. Paris: United Nations Educational, Scientific and Cultural Organisation.

Barron, I. (2009) Illegitimate participation? A group of young minority ethnic children's experience of early childhood education. *Pedagogy, Culture and Society*, 17(3), 341–354.

Bhabha, H. (1994) *The location of culture.* London: Routledge.

Bialystock, E. (2001) *Bilingualism in development: Language, literacy and cognition.* Cambridge and New York: Cambridge University Press.

Blackledge, A. & Creese, A. (2010). *Multilingualism: A critical perspective.* London: Continuum.

Bloch, D. (2007) Bilingualism: Four assumptions and four responses. *Innovation in Language Learning and Teaching*, 1(1), 66–82.

Bodrova, E. & Leong, D.J. (1996) *Tools of the mind: The Vygotskian approach to early childhood education.* Englewood Cliffs, NJ: Prentice-Hall.

Bosch, L. & Sebastian-Galles, N. (2001) Evidence of early language discrimination abilities in infants from bilingual environments. *Infancy*, 2, 29–49.

Bourdieu, P. (1977) *Outline of a theory in practice.* Cambridge: Cambridge University Press.

Brooker, L. (2003) Learning how to learn: Parental ethnotheories and young children's preparation for school. *International Journal of Early Years Education*, 11(2), 117–128.

Bucholtz, M. (2003) Sociolinguistic nostalgia and the authentication of identity. *Journal of Sociolinguistics*, 7(3), 398–416.

Chen, K.-H. (1996) The formation of a Diasporic intellectual: An interview with Stuart Hall. In K.-H. Chen and D. Morley (eds), *Stuart Hall: Critical dialogues in cultural studies* (pp. 486–505). London and New York: Routledge.

Chomsky, N. (1987) *The Chomsky reader*. Edited by James Peck. New York: Pantheon Books.

Chomsky, N. (1998) *What Uncle Sam really wants*. Berkeley, CA: Odonian Press.

Cline, T. & Frederickson, N. (eds) (1996) *Curriculum related assessment: Cummins and bilingual children*. Bristol, UK: Multilingual Matters.

Collier, V.P. (1989). How long? A synthesis of research on academic achievement in a second language. *TESOL Quarterly*, 23(3), 509–531.

Conteh, J. (2012) *Teaching bilingual and EAL learners in primary school*. London: Sage Learning Matters.

Conteh, J. & Brock, A. (2011) 'Safe spaces'? Sites of bilingualism for young learners in home, school and community. *International Journal of Bilingual Education and Bilingualism*, 14(3), 347–360.

Cope, B. & Kalantzis, M. (eds) (2000) *Multiliteracies: Literacy learning and the design of social futures*. London: Routledge.

Cowley S.J., Moodley, S. & Fiori-Cowley, A. (2004) Grounding signs of culture: Primary intersubjectivity in social semiosis. *Mind Culture and Activity*, 11, 109–132.

Creese, A. & Blackledge, A. (2010) Translanguaging in the bilingual classroom: A pedagogy for learning and teaching? *The Modern Language Journal*, 94(1), 103–115.

Cummins, J. (1984) *Bilingualism and special education*. Bristol, UK: Multilingual Matters.

Cummins, J. (1991) Interdependence of first- and second-language proficiency in bilingual children. In E. Bialystok (ed.), *Language processing in bilingual children* (pp. 70–89). Cambridge: Cambridge University Press.

Cummins, J. (1999) The ethics of doublethink: Language rights and the bilingual education debate. *TESOL Journal*, 8(3), 13–17.

Cummins, J. (2000) *Language, power, and pedagogy: Bilingual children in the crossfire*. New York: Multilingual Matters.

Cummins, J. (2001) Bilingual children's mother tongue: Why is it important for education? *Sprogforum*, 7(19), 15–20.

Cummins, J. (2015a) How to reverse a legacy of exclusion? Identifying high-impact educational responses. *Language and Education*, 29(3), 272–279.

Cummins, J. (2015b) Language differences that influence reading development: Instructional implications of alternative interpretations of the research evidence. In P. Afflerbach (ed.), *Handbook of individual differences in reading: Reader, text and context* (pp. 223–244). London and New York: Routledge.

Datta, M. (1st edn, 2000; 2nd edn, 2007) *Bilinguality and literacy: Principles and practice*. London: Continuum.

DfE (2014) *Statutory Framework for the Early Years Foundation Stage. Setting the standards for learning, development and care for children from birth to five. Published March 2014. Effective September 2014*. London: Department for Education.

Diaz, R.M. (1983) Thought and two languages: The impact of bilingualism on cognitive development. *Review of Research in Education*, 10, 23–54.

Donaldson, M. (1978) *Children's minds*. London. Fontana.

Douglas, M. (1966) *Purity and danger: An analysis of the concepts of pollution and taboo.* London and New York: Routledge.

Drury, R. (2007) *Young bilingual learners at home and school: Researching multilingual voices.* Stoke on Trent and Sterling, USA: Trentham Books.

Drury, R. (2013) How silent is the 'Silent Period' for young bilinguals in early years settings in England? *European Early Childhood Education Research Journal*, 21(3), 380–391.

Edwards, E. & Alldred, P. (2000) A typology of parental involvement in education centring on children and young people: Negotiating familialisation, institutionalisation and individualization. *British Journal of Sociology of Education*, 21(3), 435–455.

Fishman, J. (1994) *What do you lose when you lose your language?* Paper adapted from speech given by Fishman at the first Stabilising Indigenous Languages symposium in 1994. Available at: www2.nau.edu/jar/SIL/Fishman1.pdf [accessed 13 December 2015].

France, P. (1983) Working with young bilingual children. *Early Child Development and Care*, 10(4), 83–292.

France, P. & Green, T. (1978) Working with young bilingual children: An account of the ILEA's bilingual under fives project. *Early Years*, 4(1), 31–39.

Freire, P. (1985) *The politics of education: Culture, power and liberation*. New York: Berlin and Garvey.

Freire, P. (1998) *Teachers as cultural workers: Letters to those who dare teach*. Boulder, CO: Westview Press.

Garcia, O. (2009a) *Bilingual education in the 21st century: A global perspective*. New York: Blackwell/Wiley.

Garcia, O. (2009b) Keynote speech at NALDIC's 17th Annual Conference on 14 November 2009 at the University of Reading. Available at: http://bilingualeducation translanguaging.bravesites.com/ofelia-garcia-you-tube-links [accessed 7 December 2015].

Goldberg, D.T. (1993) *Racist culture: Philosophy and the politics of meaning*. Chichester, UK: Wiley-Blackwell.

Gort, M. & Pontier, R.W. (2012) Exploring bilingual pedagogies in dual language preschool classrooms. *Language and Education*, 10, 1–23.

Gratier, M. (2003) Expressive timing and interactional synchrony between mothers and infants: Cultural similarities, cultural differences, and the immigration experience. *Cognitive Development*, 18(4), 533–554.

Gratier, M. & Trevarthen, C. (2007) Voice, vitality and meaning: On the shape of the infant's utterances in willing engagement with culture. Comment on Bertau's 'On the Notion of Voice'. *International Journal for Dialogical Science*, 2(1), 169–181.

Grosjean, F. (1982) *Life with two languages: An introduction to bilingualism*. Cambridge, MA: Harvard University Press.

Grosjean, F. (1985) The bilingual as a competent but specific speaker-hearer. *Journal of Multilingual and Multicultural Development*, 6(6), 467–477.

Gutiérrez, K. (2008) Developing a sociocritical literacy in the third space. *Reading Research Quarterly*, 43(2), 148–164.

Gutiérrez, K.D, Larson, J. & Kreuter, B. (1995) Script, counterscript and underlife in the classroom: James Brown versus Brown v. Board of Education. *Harvard Educational Review*, 65(3), 445–471.

Gutiérrez, K.D., Baquedano-López, P. & Tejeda, C. (1999) Rethinking diversity: Hybridity and hybrid language practices in the third space. *Mind, Culture, and Activity*, 6(4), 286–303.

Hall, D., Griffiths, D., Haslam, L. & Wilkin, Y. (2001) *Assessing the needs of bilingual pupils: Living in two languages*. London: David Fulton.

Hall, K.A., Özerk, K., Zulfiqar, M. & Tan, J.E.C. (2002) 'This is our school': Provision, purpose and pedagogy of supplementary schooling in Leeds and Oslo. *British Educational Research Journal*, 28(2), 399–418.

Hall, S. (1997) *Race, the floating signifier.* Transcript of a lecture he gave at Goldsmiths College in London, published by the Media Education Foundation, 60 Masonic St., Northampton.

Hall, S. and Adams, T. (2007) 'Cultural hallmark'. [Stuart Hall interviewed] by Tim Adams. *The Observer*, Sunday 23 September 2007. Available at: www.theguardian.com/society/2007/sep/23/communities.politicsphilosophyandsociety [accessed 7 December 2015].

Hamirani, K. (n.d.) Quoted on website: http://childrens-research-centre.open.ac.uk [accessed 13 December 2015].

Harrop-Allin, S. (2014) 'The pen talks my story': South African children's multimodel storytelling as artistic practice. In A. Archer and D. Newfield (eds), *Multimodal approaches to research and pedagogy: Recognition, resources and access.* New York and London: Routledge.

Haworth, P., Cullen, J., Simmons, H., Schimanski, L., McGarva, P. & Woodhead, E. (2006) The role of acquisition and learning in young children's bilingual development: A sociocultural interpretation. *International Journal of Bilingual Education and Bilingualism*, 9(3), 295–309, DOI: 10.1080/13670050608668651.

Heath, S.B. (1983) *Ways with words: Language, life and work in communities and classrooms.* Cambridge and New York: Cambridge University Press.

Heath, S.B. (2010) Family literacy or community learning? Some critical questions on perspective. In K. Dunsmore and D. Fisher (eds), *Bringing Literacy Home.* Newark, DE: International Reading Association.

Hornberger, N. & Link, H. (2012) Translanguaging and transnational literacies in multilingual classrooms: A biliteracy lens. *International Journal of Bilingual Education and Bilingualism*, 15(3), 261–278.

Issa, T. & Hatt, A. (2013) *Language, culture and identity in the early years.* London: Bloomsbury.

Jewitt, C. (2009). An introduction to multimodality. In C. Jewitt (ed.), *The Routledge handbook of multimodal analysis* (pp. 14–27). New York: Routledge.

Kenner, C. (2004a) Living in simultaneous worlds: Difference and integration in bilingual script-learning. *International Journal of Bilingual Education and Bilingualism*, 7(1), 43–61.

Kenner, C. (2004b) *Becoming biliterate: Young children learning different writing systems.* Stoke on Trent, UK: Trentham Books.

Kenner, C. & Mahera, R. (2013) Connecting children's worlds: Creating a multilingual syncretic curriculum in partnership with complementary schools. *Journal of Early Childhood Literacy*, 13(3), 395–417.

King, K. & Mackey, A. (2007) *The bilingual edge: Why, when, and how to teach your child a second language.* New York: HarperCollins.

Kitoko Nsiku, K. (2007) Dogs' languages or people's languages? The return of Bantu languages to primary schools in Mozambique. *Current Issues in Language Planning,* 8(2), 258–282.

Krashen, S.D. (1988) *Second language acquisition and second language learning.* Upper Saddle River, NJ: Prentice-Hall.

Kress, G. (1997) *Before writing: Rethinking the paths to literacy.* London and New York: Routledge.

Kurban, F. & Tobin, J. (2009) 'They don't like us': Reflections of Turkish children in a German preschool. *Contemporary Issues in Early Childhood,* 10, 24–34.

Lao, C. (2004) Parents' attitudes towards Chinese-English bilingual education and Chinese-language use. *Bilingual Research Journal,* 28(1), 99–120.

Leung, C., Harris, R., & Rampton, B. (1997) The idealised native speaker, reified ethnicities and classroom realities. *TESOL Quarterly,* 31(3), 543–560.

Levi, P. (1979) *The truce.* London: Abacus.

Levi, P. (1989) *The drowned and the saved.* London: Michael Joseph.

Lewis, G., Jones, B. & Baker, C. (2012) Translanguaging: Developing its conceptualisation and contextualisation. *Educational Research and Evaluation: An International Journal on Theory and Practice,* 18(7), 655–670.

Lightbown, P.M. (2008) Easy as pie? Children learning languages. *Concordia Working Papers in Applied Linguistics,* 1, 1–25.

López-Robertson, J. & Schramm-Pate, S. (2013) (Un)official knowledge and identity: An emerging bilingual's journey into hybridity. *Innovation in Language Learning and Teaching,* 7(1), 40–56.

Macedo, D. & Bartolome, L. (2014) Multiculturalism permitted in English only. *International Multilingual Research Journal,* 8, 24–37.

Macrory, G. (2006) Bilingual language development: What do early years practitioners need to know? *Early Years: An International Research Journal,* 26(2), 159–169.

Malloch, S. & Trevarthen, C. (2009) Musicality: Communicating the vitality and interests of life. In S. Malloch and C. Trevarthen, *Communicative musicality: Exploring the basis of human companionship* (pp. 1–12). Oxford: Oxford University Press.

Maylor, U., Glass, K., Issa, T., Kuyok, K., Kuyok, A., Minty, S., Rose, A. & Ross, A.: Institute for Policy Studies in Education, London Metropolitan University. Tanner, E., Finch, S., Low, N. Taylor. E. & Tipping, S.: National Centre for Social Research. Purdon, S. & Purdon, B.: Social Research (2010) *Impact of supplementary schools on pupils' attainment: An investigation into what factors contribute to educational improvements.* Institute for Policy Studies in Education, London Metropolitan University.

Mehler, J., Jusczyk, P.W., Lambertz, G., Halsted, N., Bertoncini, J. & Amiel-Tison, C. (1988) A precursor of language acquisition in young infants. *Cognition,* 29, 143–178.

Miller, J. (1983) *Many voices: Bilingualism, culture, and education.* London and Boston: Routledge & Kegan Paul.

Miller, J.M. (2003) *Audible difference: ESL and social identity in schools.* Bristol, UK: Multilingual Matters.

Ministry of Education (1996) *Te Whāriki: Early childhood curriculum.* Wellington: Learning Media.

Ministry of Education (2002) *Pathways to the future: Nga Huaraki Arataki. A 10-year strategic plan for early childhood education.* Wellington: Learning Media.

Moje, E.B., Ciechanowski, K.M., Ellis, L., Carrillo, R. & Collazo, T. (2004) Working toward third space in content area literacy: An examination of everyday funds of knowledge and discourse. *Reading Research Quarterly*, 39(3), 38–70.

Mushi, S. (2002a) Simultaneous and successive second language learning: Integral ingredients of the human development process. *Early Child Development and Care*, 172(4), 349–358.

Mushi, S. (2002b) Acquisition of multiple languages among children of immigrant families: Parents' role in the home-school language pendulum. *Early Child Development and Care*, 172(5), 517–530.

Myers-Scotton, C. (2005) *Multiple voices: An introduction to bilingualism.* Oxford: Blackwell.

Nsamenang, A.B. & Lamb, M.E. (1998) Socialization of Nso children in the Bamenda Grassfields of Northwest Cameroon in Woodhead. In D. Faulkner and K. Littleton (eds), *Cultural worlds of early childhood* (pp. 250–261). London and New York: Routledge and The Open University.

Nsamenang, A.B. & Tchombe, T. (eds) (2011) *Handbook of African educational theories and practices: A generative teacher education curriculum.* Bamenda, Cameroon: Human Development Resource Centre.

Pacini-Ketchabaw, V. & Armstrong de Almeida, A. (2006) Language discourses and ideologies at the heart of early childhood education. *International Journal of Bilingual Education and Bilingualism*, 9(3), 310–341.

Parke, T. & Drury, R. (2001) Language development at home and school: Gains and losses in young bilinguals. *Early Years: An International Research Journal*, 21(2), 117–127.

Pollard, A., Anderson, J., Maddock, M., Swaffield, S., Warin, J. & Warwick, P. (2008) *Reflective teaching: Evidence-informed professional practice* (3rd edn). London: Continuum.

Rich, S. & Davis, L. (2007) Insights into the strategic ways in which two bilingual children in the early years seek to negotiate the competing demands on their identity in their home and school worlds. *International Journal of Early Years Education*, 15(1), 35–47.

Select Committee on Race Relations and Immigration (SCRRI) (1977) *The West Indian community.* Report with minutes of proceedings and appendices v. 1 (House of Commons Papers). London: HMSO.

Semali, L. & Kinchloe, J. (eds) (1999) *What is indigenous knowledge and why should we study it?* New York: Basic Books.

Skutnabb-Kangas, T. & Cummins, J. (eds) (1988) *Minority education: From shame to struggle.* Bristol, UK and Philadelphia: Multilingual Matters.

Smidt, S. (2001) 'All stories that have happy endings have a bad character': A young child responds to televisual texts in *English in Education. NATE*, 35(2), 25–34.

Smidt, S. (2008) *Supporting multilingual learners in the early years: Many languages – many children.* London and New York: Routledge.

Smidt, S. (2009) *Introducing Vygotsky.* London and New York: Routledge.

Smidt, S. (ed.) (2010) *Key issues in early years education* (2nd edn). London and New York: Routledge.

Smidt, S. (2011) *Introducing Bruner.* London and New York: Routledge.

Smidt, S. (2013a) *Introducing Malaguzzi*. London and New York: Routledge.

Smidt, S. (2013b) *The developing child in the 21st century: A global perspective on child development*. London and New York: Routledge.

Smith, M. (1931) A study of five bilingual children from the same family. *Child Development*, 2, 184–187.

Sneddon, R. (2000) Language and literacy: Children's experiences in multilingual environments. *International Journal of Bilingual Education and Bilingualism*, 3(4), 265–282.

Sneddon, R. (2010) ABETARE and dancing. In V. Lytra and P. Martin (eds), *Sites of multilingualism: Complementary schools in Britain to-day*. Stoke on Trent, UK: Trentham Books.

Thompson, L. (2000) *Young bilingual children in nursery school*. Bristol, UK: Multilingual Matters.

Travers, P., Klein, G. & Wiles, S. (2004) *Equal measures: Ethnic minority and bilingual pupils in secondary schools*. Stoke on Trent: Trentham Books.

UN Convention on the Rights of the Child (UNCRC) (1989), UK: UNICEF. Available at: www.unicef.org.uk/UNICEFs-Work/UN-Convention/ [accessed 9 December 2015].

Voss, B. (2010) Supporting young children. In S. Smidt (ed.), *Key issues in early years education* (2nd edn). London and New York: Routledge.

Vygotsky, L.S. (1978) *Mind in society: The development of higher psychological processes*. Cambridge, MA: Harvard University Press.

Wa Thiong'o, N. (1986) *Decolonising the mind: The politics of language in African literature*. Portsmouth, NH: Heinemann Press.

Wells, G. (1986) *The meaning makers: Learning to talk and talking to learn*. Bristol, UK: Multilingual Matters.

Wiles, S. (1979) Working with young bilingual children. *Early Development and Care*, 10(4), 284.

Williams, C. (1994) *Report to the Welsh Assembly* (1994) Available at: www.legislation. gov.uk/ukpga/1994/19/contents [accessed 7 December 2015].

Woodhead, M. (2005) Early childhood development: A question of rights. *International Journal of Early Childhood*, 37(3), 79–98.

Official documents and websites

National Curriculum in England, framework for key stages 1 to 4: www.gov.uk/national-curriculum

EYFS Statutory Framework: www.foundationyears.org.uk/eyfs-statutory-framework/

The Rampton Report (1981): *West Indian Children in our Schools*: www.educationengland. org.uk/documents/rampton/

The Swann Report (1985): *Education for All*: www.educationengland.org.uk/documents/swann/swann1985.html

Local Government (Wales) Act (1984): www.legislation.gov.uk/ukpga/1994/19/contents

The Open University's Children's Research Centre: http://childrens-research-centre. open.ac.uk

Ofelia Garcia's 'Education, multilingualism and translanguaging in the 21st century': https://ofeliagarciadotorg.files.wordpress.com/2011/02/education-multilingualism-translanguaging-21st-century.pdf

UN Convention on the Rights of the Child (1989), UNICEF UK: www.unicef.org.uk/UNICEFs-Work/UN-Convention/

The Rampton Report (1981)
West Indian Children in our Schools
Interim report of the Committee of Inquiry into the Education of Children from Ethnic Minority Groups.
London: Her Majesty's Stationery Office 1981.
© Crown copyright material is reproduced with the permission of the Controller of HMSO and the Queen's Printer for Scotland.

The Swann Report (1985)
Education for All
Report of the Committee of Enquiry into the Education of Children from Ethnic Minority Groups.
London: Her Majesty's Stationery Office 1985.
© Crown copyright material is reproduced with the permission of the Controller of HMSO and the Queen's Printer for Scotland.

Education for All (EFA) is a global movement led by UNESCO (United Nation Educational, Scientific and Cultural Organization), aiming to meet the learning needs of all children, youth and adults by 2015.

The Bullock Report (1975)
A Language for Life
Report of the Committee of Enquiry appointed by the Secretary of State for Education and Science under the Chairmanship of Sir Alan Bullock FBA.
London: Her Majesty's Stationery Office 1975.
© Crown copyright material is reproduced with the permission of the Controller of HMSO and the Queen's Printer for Scotland.

Statutory Framework for the Early Years Foundation Stage. Setting the standards for learning, development and care for children from birth to five. Published March 2014. Effective September 2014. London: Department for Education.

Index

The chapter headings/topics are in **bold text**.